Psychology of Terrorists

Profiling and CounterAction

Dr. Raymond H. Hamden
Clinical and Forensic Psychologist
Consultant in Political Psychology
* * * * *

Fellow, American Academy of Forensic Sciences (Psychiatry & Behavioral Sciences Section)

Executive Director, The Foundation For International Human Relations

Board of Directors, Swiss Middle Eastern Alliance (SwissMEA)

Life Member of the Association of Psychological Sciences, International Society of Political Psychology, International Council of Psychologists

Foreword by Dr Henry C. Lee, Forensic Scientist

Psychology of Terrorists

Profiling and CounterAction

Raymond H. Hamden

CRC Press
Taylor & Francis Group
Boca Raton London New York

CRC Press is an imprint of the
Taylor & Francis Group, an **informa** business

CRC Press
Taylor & Francis Group
6000 Broken Sound Parkway NW, Suite 300
Boca Raton, FL 33487-2742

© 2019 by Taylor & Francis Group, LLC
CRC Press is an imprint of Taylor & Francis Group, an Informa business

No claim to original U.S. Government works

Printed on acid-free paper

International Standard Book Number-13: 978-1-4398-1002-6 (Hardback)

Visit the Taylor & Francis Web site at
http://www.taylorandfrancis.com

and the CRC Press Web site at
http://www.crcpress.com

For a better world, this document is offered

To my family:
spouse, children, grandchildren,
brothers, nieces and nephews, cousins,
their respective spouses, and parents

To the good people of this planet
who work to make a better distinction for all
in the interest of a
world for the common good of all humankind

Contents

Foreword

There are many reasons why an individual or organization may engage in acts of terrorism, some of which have been uncovered through psycho-social investigations, rendering politics, economics, religion, and academics among those factors. To understand the *Psychology of Terrorists* is to realize the making of the troubled world with people who seek human rights of respected recognition, the pursuit of prosperity, in the quest of exhilaration.

Dr. Raymond Hamden expects a unique readership; one that, in the name of academics, puts aside any prejudices and biases into which they may have been born and socially influenced, in order to better understand the reasons behind criminality and terrorism.

In this text we learn that labeling individuals as *the other* or *the terrorist* based only on processes of categorization in terms of race, creed, nationality, religion, socioeconomic status, or any other factors commonly used today, is an act of discrimination that is similar to the very crime we fight when combating fundamentalists or extremists of terrorist actions. Consistently keeping in mind that no one has the right to an opinion until all sides are heard allows professional investigators an opportunity to seek the truth, a process that can never be one-sided. Professionals of any field of practice, more specifically those in law enforcement and psychology, have a mandate to protect society rather than contaminate a community and nation with unsubstantiated answers.

The chapter topics of this text provide the reader with an opportunity to gain knowledge and information alongside guided experience and skills in order to develop the application needed to profile and to counteract what is truly categorized as dreadful behaviors. Validity and reliability are found with sound evidence gained in a scientific manner. Therefore, justified conviction of terrorist crimes can only be correctly achieved when standardized accuracy is realized via a balanced collection of facts.

It is important to note that counteraction in this text refers to *negotiations in general*, and not what may be interpreted as counter-terrorism. To seek a solution is to negotiate, thus this document stresses conflict resolution with added sensitivity and a focus on cross-cultural negotiations to gain the truth.

Little, if any, has previously been written on the types of terrorists featured in this text. Initiation of the forthcoming information is based on research and consultations conducted by Dr. Hamden while serving as a 1986 Visiting Fellow at the Center for International Development and Conflict Management at the University of Maryland–College Park.

The tools for profiling provided in this document are suggestions for the professional to select the items that would be applicable in each scenario. With experience, an expert may develop their own preferred style or maintain the flexibility to adjust to the many differing circumstances that arise. Though it is difficult to standardize behavior, since it is greatly influenced by individual dispositions and environmental circumstances, and varies from one person to another, intensive and collaborated research can potentially lead us to a time when a standard assessment and profiling criteria would apply to all acts of terrorism and the individual terrorist. This concept is beyond risk assessment, yet combined with this profiling intervention, the two will complement the expectations, goals, and aims to be achieved.

Dr. Hamden leads the work on identifying four types of terrorists, among them are extremists he refers to be Ethnogeographic Political and Ethnogeographic Religious. Yet, there are the individuals who have premorbid characteristics of psychopathology (forensic terminology) or antisocial personality disorder (clinical terminology). The fourth type is the Retributional Terrorist, a term he coined through differential research and application.

The 3Is, mentioned in this text are related mostly to the extremists who want to impress, impose, and implement their chosen ideology on people, society, and the world-at-large. This work is noteworthy in bringing to the forefront some characteristics of behavior, which law enforcement can find to qualify two of the four types of terrorists.

"Tract II: Profiling and CounterAction" (Chapter 11) is highlighted here with the opportunity to apply the techniques with training programs. The work being performed in profiling meets many obstacles—access to those accused of the acts of terror, willingness to discuss the action for which they are accused, true evidence to be shared by the law enforcement agencies, racial prejudices, or limited understanding of mind-set and behavior with a focus only on violent and extremist individuals or groups

Congratulations to Dr. Hamden for these contributions in profiling. I look forward to further studies and training programs to advance this important area.

Dr. Henry C. Lee
Chair Professor in Forensic Science
University of New Haven
Connecticut

Author

Raymond H. Hamden, PhD, earned a PhD in psychology in 1977 and continued postgraduate studies at the Philadelphia School of Modern Psychoanalysis, Pennsylvania (1980). His postdoctoral fellowship in political psychology was held at the University of Maryland, Center for International Development & Conflict Management (CIDCM) in 1986.

He is a consultant in clinical and forensic psychology, political psychology, profiling, crisis intervention, trauma, and homeland security; and holds diplomate status and fellow status in professional organizations by peer review and examination.

A member of Infragard, Dr. Hamden resides in the United States and continues to work as a presenter, consultant, and mentor to academia, corporations, and media, globally.

With four decades of studying and practicing psychology in the United States and the Middle East and North Africa (MENA), he has published in peer-reviewed journals, presented before U.S. Congress by invitation, served as chair on professional committees by government summons, and has consulted in more than 30 nations in the areas of clinical, forensic, and political psychology, with the working application of diversity and inclusion for all cultures.

Contributions in Forensic Psychology

Forensic Psychology in the UAE. 2015. *UAE Psychologist Newsletter*, Vol 5, May–December, pp. 5, 14.

Psychology of Terrorists: 4 Types [New Dimensions]. November 7, 2015. North Shore Long Island Jewish Hospital, Keynote Address at the Perioperative Nursing Conference.

Psychology Perspective on Elderly Abuse. October 2014. Lecture/Workshop, Arnold Markle Symposium, Henry C. Lee Institute of Forensic Sciences, University of New Haven, Connecticut.

True Faces of Terrorists. February 2014. Seminar, American Academy of Forensic Sciences Conference, Seattle, Washington.

New Dimensions in Profiling Terrorists. December 2013. Keynote Address at the ASIS 7th Asia-Pacific Security Forum, Macau, China.

Perspective on Profiling Offenders: Interview with Alleged Offenders and Prevention October 2013. Workshop, Arnold Markle Symposium, Henry C. Lee Institute of Forensic Sciences, University of New Haven, Connecticut.

HEDAYAH (Abu Dhabi) led a *Closed Meeting of Experts of Psychology in Rehabilitation of Violent Extremists* in collaboration with the United Nations Interregional Crime and Justice Research Institute (UNICRI); the International Center for Counter Terrorism (ICCT), The Hague; the Bureau of Counterterrorism, U.S. Department of State and invited Dr. Hamden to be a participant in this post hoc to the Rome Memorandum on Good Practices for Rehabilitation and Reintegration of Violent Extremist Offenders.

Dr. Hamden was a 1986 visiting fellow at the Center for International Development and Conflict Management. His research and consulting was in Political Psychology—The Psychology of Terrorists and Hostage Situations. He coined the term the *Retributional Terrorist—Type 4.*

"The Retributional Terrorist—Type 4." 2002. Chapter in a four-volume text entitled *The Psychology of Terrorism,* edited by Dr. Chris Stout.

"Unresolved Trauma and the Thirst for Revenge: The Retributional Terrorist." 2005. Chapter in Volume I of a three-volume project entitled *The Making of a Terrorist,* edited by Dr. James J.F. Forest, West Point United States Military Academy.

By invitation, Dr. Hamden presented before the U.S. Senate and wrote for the U.S. House of Representatives:

Psychological Aspects of IsTishHad: Suicide or Sacrifice. March 26, 1986. Expert witness testimony presented before the U.S. Senate Anti-Terrorism Caucus, special topic on the Middle East suicide missions, Washington, DC.

Islamic Fundamentalism: Terrorism or Psychological Resistance. Fall/Winter 1985. Written testimony submitted to and published in the series of HEARINGS before the Subcommittee on Europe and the Middle East of the Committee on Foreign Affairs, U.S. House of Representatives, Washington, DC, pp. 416–425.

Acknowledgments

When conducting research, a lot of information is availed on a daily basis; this can be seen in any field of study. Topics such as terrorism, terrorists, psychological profiling, intelligence analysis, negotiations, and counter-terrorism also require further reading and assistance.

The individuals named here were most helpful to enhancing the quality of the training tools tested with peers of various expertise—law enforcement, homeland security, forensic scientists, academics, business people, behavioral science and mental health, medical and neurosciences.

Acknowledgment and appreciation goes to those who gave of their time, knowledge, and skills during the preparation of this text.

Research and Contributions

Hend Abdel Sattar, MA, Criminology and Criminal Justice, City University College, London, United Kingdom, reviewed and confirmed research references. She also contributed to the balance of information and thoughtful understanding of potential explanations to each concept presented.

Danielle Graddick and *Elizabeth Turner*, Wright State University, Dayton, Ohio, PsyD candidates, assisted with research and the preliminary writings on the four types of terrorists.

Alisha Fernandes, MSc, Applied Psychology, Middlesex University, Dubai, United Arab Emirates campus, and PsyM, Clinical Psychology, Wright State University, Dayton, Ohio, was primarily responsible for research confirmation and editing the chapters "Psychopathic Terrorists," "Techniques of Intervention," and "Track I: Profiling and Counter-Terrorism," and reviewing "History of Terrorists in Brief."

Aroushi Malhotra, MA, Management and Psychology, University of St. Andrews, Fife, United Kingdom, was primarily responsible for research confirmation and editing the chapter "Techniques of Interviews and Interrogations." She also added the "Effects of Mass Media on Terrorism" section to the chapter "Understanding Terrorist Attacks: Methods, Mode, Tactics, and Strategies."

Midhat Fatema, BSc, Psychology with Counseling Skills, Middlesex University, Dubai, United Arab Emirates campus and currently matriculated as an MSc candidate in Psychological Counseling at the Indian Institute of Psychology and Research, Bangalore, was primarily responsible for research confirmation and editing the chapters "Analysis with Psychological Defense Styles," "Retributional Terrorists," and "Understanding Terrorist Attacks: Methods, Mode, Tactics, and Strategies."

Maria Christine L. Basilio, MA, Psychology, Ateneo de Manila University, Philippines, was primarily responsible for research confirmation and editing the chapter "Ethnogeographic Terrorists: Religious and Political," as well as adding valuable material to the "Profiling Strategies" section in the chapter "Track II: Profiling and CounterAction."

Dr. Omar Kader earned a double-major undergraduate degree from Brigham Young University, an MA in political science, and a PhD in international relations from the University of Southern California. In 1986, during our Washington, DC brainstorming meetings on topics of mutual interest and research in terrorist psychology, he was influential in naming the fourth type of terrorist, retributional.

Final Draft Proof Reader

Najdia Diane Kiblinger, University of Houston, Texas
Trusted for review and critique on text presentation
Precious daughter of this author

Academic Field Trials for Training and Presentation to Peers

- World Federation for Mental Health
- American Academy of Forensic Sciences
- Henry C. Lee Institute of Forensic Sciences
- University of New Haven, Connecticut
- MENA Regional Conference of Psychology, Jordan
- American Society for Industrial Security (ASIS) International
- International Society of Political Psychology
- Middlesex University Graduate School, Dubai Campus
- Duke University Field Study in Washington, DC

Technical Assistance and Review

The statistical applications were performed by *Elena Maria Andriotis*, MSc, Clinical Psychology, and PhD, Psychology, United Kingdom.

Proofreading and research confirmation were performed by *Gerlie Saura* of Italy, *Karishma Kewalram* from Singapore, and *Jodie Danielle Palmer* from the United Kingdom. Script proofreading was assisted by *Donna O'Neil* of Tennessee and *Camilla O. Rantsen* of California.

Anna Karmandarian kindly offered guidance on the general topic and potential applications for training. Her expertise as monitor and evaluator in health and education was appreciated.

The multilingual *Reem Rabia* of Canada, a participating observer at presentations, confirmed interpretations in English, French, and Arabic when needed, to monitor the development and audience responses of the program on the psychology of terrorists.

Nancy Yamout, MBA, MSW, and *Maya Yamout*, MBA, MSW, field workers from the Modern University for Business and Science, Beirut, Lebanon, led the daring march of prisoner reform for those accused of terrorist acts. They established RescueME in Lebanon in 2011, a nongovernmental organization that offers children and youth an education and training for a productive life alternative rather than recruitment into the destruction of terrorism and continuing research until present inside a prison. This author is grateful to both for initiating and managing the case studies that contributed to the research.

To test the subject of *Psychology of Terrorists: Profiling and CounterAction*, presentation opportunities in the United States and at international conferences were granted.

In the United States

Lecture and workshop programs on the topic of psychology of terrorists were presented at the conferences of the American Academy of Forensic Sciences, American Board of Certification in Homeland Security, American Psychotherapy Association, and North Shore Long Island Jewish Hospital at the Perioperative Nursing Conference (2015).

International Locations

Under the auspices of the International Union of Psychological Sciences, International Association of Applied Psychology, and International Association for Cross-Cultural Psychology, this topic was a workshop/seminar at the Southeastern European Regional Conference on Psychology (SEE-RCP) in Bulgaria in 2009, The Second Middle East North Africa Regional Conference on Psychology (MENA-RCP) held in Jordan in 2007, and the First Middle East North Africa Regional Conference on Psychology (MENA-RCP) held in Dubai in 2003.

As a seminar, "Psychology of Terrorists" was presented at the 2008 Science Po Conference of the International Society of Political Psychology in France. In 2007, this seminar was presented to the Rajasthan Department of Police, Jaipur, India.

This and a related topic were this author's keynote address at the American Society for Industrial Security (ASIS) conference in Dubai (2009) and in Macau (2013).

Invited to participate in a post hoc select assembly to the Rome Memorandum on Good Practices for Rehabilitation and Reintegration of Violent Extremist

Offenders, "Closed Meeting of Experts of Psychology in Rehabilitation of Violent Extremists," in collaboration with the United Nations Interregional Crime and Justice Research Institute (UNICRI), the International Center for Counter-Terrorism (ICCT), The Hague, and the Bureau of Counterterrorism of the U.S. Department of State (hosted by Hedayah, May 2013, in Abu Dhabi, United Arab Emirates).

Special recognition is given to various agencies and organizations in America, Europe, the Middle East, and Asia that shared information, availed data, and supported access to individuals whose participation contributed to this work. Names and locations are respectfully kept confidential to protect privacy and prevent disclosure.

Gratitude is expressed to the individuals named above, professional organizations, and their respective executives and program committees, for their consideration and availing the Psychology of Terrorists program for peer review. Gratitude is also expressed to the students and professional participants who kindly gave their objective critique to enrich the standard of knowledge and skills for application to the *Psychology of Terrorists: Profiling and CounterAction.*

Chapter 1

History of Terrorists in Brief

Contrary to popular thought, the concept of terrorism is older than any modern nation as we know it. Still, it is not fully understood how this concept works, or how the idea is represented and utilized, both by governments and those acting against certain governments. Terrorism, as a phenomenon, rears its ugly head through a vast array of tactical methods, causing physical and/or psychological damage, occurring in the physical and/or the cyber world, and is guided by a wide range of ideologies, be they political, religious, or philosophical. As such, a sole understanding of the term *terrorism* will not do it justice. There are many legal, moral, and ethical debates that we as a society regularly engage in, as a result of terrorism. For instance, are environmentalists who take up arms considered terrorists or freedom fighters? How do we categorize Ted Kaczynski (aka the Unabomber)? Can we compare him to the French revolutionaries who fought to bring about awareness of a long-needed social and political reform? Or does he fall more in line with the Baader-Meinhof Gang (aka the Red Army Faction), who are characterized as a radical group responsible for mass and serial crimes while similarly fighting for political changes?

In order for us to be able to distinctly categorize what is or is not perceived as terror, we tend to use morality as our guide. Utilizing such a basis for judgment may at times support the argument. However, it may also serve to severely hamper our ability to recognize and place higher emphasis on the act of terrorism itself rather than focusing solely on the consequences. Is a car bomb more likely to be perceived as an act of terrorism than military action causing multiple civilian deaths? Both acts include innocent civilian deaths as a consequence, along with fear and destruction—all buzzwords for terrorism; nonetheless, each act can be, and is, interpreted and represented differently in our world today.

> *One man's terrorist is another man's freedom fighter.*

We are prompted to question whether military action is terrorism concealed beneath a different name or if this is simply the justification that most violent terrorists cling to? Those wanting to disrupt order and peace are creatively and constantly finding new ways to do so, thus allowing the definition of *terrorism* to continue to broaden over time. Over the last two decades, the world has seen terrorism and violence escalate. As such, more research and studies are required to gain a better understanding of the reasons behind it, as positive attempts to find solutions and enhance prevention.

Terrorism adheres to both left- and right-wing ideologies. On one side, we witness the Marxists, and on the other, the dictatorships and states built primarily on business leadership. Nationalists are often involved in causes protecting members of a cultural group or a certain region, while religious extremists are fighting for the supremacy of their religion and tend to view anything modern as immoral, a threat to their beliefs, and something that must be destroyed. Meanwhile, special-interest groups are taking arms against world phenomena such as abortion, animal rights, and the destruction of the environment—all following the consequentialist standpoint where the ends justify the means.

Overview of Terrorism

Terrorism can be defined as the systematic and calculated use of violence, or simply the threat of violence, against individuals in order to obtain a certain goal. This goal can be political, ideological, or religious in nature, and is usually achieved by instilling outstanding pressure, intimidation, and fear (Terrorism, 2018). It is most commonly believed that terrorism is a definition for situations that are intended to create immense fear and ones that show no empathy for civilians and anybody who intervenes. Not only is the term *terrorism* viewed as basic unconventional warfare, but also, because it has a strong impact and influence, both politically and emotionally, it is viewed as a form of psychological warfare. A 1988 U.S. Army study found that there are more than 100 definitions for terrorism, and it very succinctly labeled any person who practices terrorism a "terrorist."

An International Round Table on Constructing Peace, Deconstructing Terror (2004), hosted by the Strategic Foresight Group, called for a distinction between terrorism and acts of terror. Per United Nations Security Council Resolution 1373 (2001), acts of terrorism are criminal acts. There is a global consensus that acts of terrorism should continue to be absolutely unacceptable. However, what we deem as terrorism continues to be a point of contention. This matter is brought up at major important conventions, such as the United Nations Counter-Terrorism Strategy, the Madrid Conference on Terrorism, the Strategic Foresight Group, and the ALDE Round Tables at the European Parliament. However, no consensus has been reached to better clarify the term and the acts that fall beneath it.

Origin of the Term *Terrorism*

The term *terrorism*, as we know it, dates back to 1795. It was then used as a description for the actions of the Jacobin Club in their rule of post-revolutionary France, known as the "Reign of Terror." Their justification of violence that escalated over time was to bring about political and cultural change; though the club did eventually close, they have had a strong influence throughout history and a strong impact on how we view and characterize terrorism.

Maximilien Robespierre, a deputy and member of the Committee of Public Safety in the 1970s, and one of the most famous and influential figures of the French Revolution, was very strong and instrumental during this Reign of Terror. According to his speech at the French National Convention in 1794, "If the basis of a popular government in peacetime is virtue, its basis in a time of revolution is virtue and terror-virtue, without which terror would be barbaric; and terror, without which virtue would be impotent." This made him among the very first individuals within the political or governmental sphere to legitimize the use of violence. Robespierre was himself a victim of his own "system" and was eventually arrested and executed. Even until today, politicians and governments assess and characterize terrorism in accordance to their own views and goals.

Agencies, experts, and governments have not been able to reach a consensus to define *terrorism*, but many have established broad or basic definitions. For instance, the United Nations Security Council report (United Nations, 2004) described terrorism as "intended to cause death or serious bodily harm to civilians or noncombatants with the purpose of intimidating a population or compelling a government or an international organization to do or abstain from doing any act."

Others, such as the U.S. Department of Defense (DoD), countered with their own definition: "The calculated use of unlawful violence or threat of unlawful violence to inculcate fear; intended to coerce or to intimidate governments or societies in the pursuit of goals that are generally political, religious, or ideological" (Departments of the Army and Air Force, 1990; Department of Defense, 2010). The primary difference between the two definitions is that the United States deems "fear" as sufficient to label the act as "terrorism," while the United Nations requires more concrete consequences, including bodily harm or death of civilians.

Differences between Criminals and Terrorists

Given that criminals who kill people and terrorists both pose physical threats to society, it is quite easy to conflate the two terms and suggest that terrorists are merely criminals. However, it is important to determine the forces that drive these individuals to kill others. Upon examining around 400 cases, Holmes and

Deburger (1998) suggested that criminals who kill others can be categorized into four types:

The hedonistic type—This type engages in the act of killing another purely to achieve the thrill from the act. Typically, the hedonistic killer gains pleasure from killing others.

The power/controlling type—This type of killer is typically one to engage in sexual assaults, whereby he is the one in control, while the victim is powerless to stop him. The controlling type of killer derives his pleasure from being in a position of power to do as he pleases to the victim, who he perceives to be helpless.

The visionary—This type of killer is one who kills because he hears "voices," possibly from God or a demon, which directs him to engage in the act of killing. These voices are likely due to the killer experiencing hallucinations of delusions, typically found in psychotic disorders.

The missionary—This type of killer is motivated by a mission to kill others, specifically to kill certain groups of people, be they a specific race, gender, or other group.

However, unlike criminals, terrorists are driven by other factors that motivate them to cause harm to others. Terrorist behavior can be explained through the 3I model:

■ *Impress*—Terrorists tend to impress their beliefs and radical thoughts upon people of similar demography
■ *Impose*—Terrorists choose to impose their ideology on the community at large
■ *Implement*—Terrorists would like to implement their concept of rule and order upon the world at large

When conducting a differential assessment of crime, defining the 3Is may be key to determine whether the act is one of terror or crime, which may have no purpose to impress, impose, or implement.

Criminals may commit acts of crime yet have no purpose outside their own impulsive gratification, monetary, or materialistic desire. Terrorists, particularly ethnogeographic and retribution types, will have a defined goal with defined aims.

Psychologists may have an explanation for human actions,
but there is never an excuse to do harm.

Revisiting the history of individuals of terror may enlighten us of their motivation, conscious, or unconscious. The conscious is our awareness and we can control what we know. The unconscious is what actually motivates our behavior according to psychoanalytic writings. It is our unawareness and we cannot control that which we are not mindful of.

Terrorism typically involves causing physical harm or the threat of violence, usually to induce a sense of fear within the community at large. These terror attacks or threats are made to coerce people to take action or prevent them from taking action, such as influencing a political policy, for example, a terrorist attack on a family planning clinic that allows families to have abortions or birth control. Moreover, terrorist attacks are typically violent and directed toward civilians, usually in public areas, to achieve a public audience; the greater the media coverage of the attack, the better the publicity for the terrorist cause. It should be noted that while violent criminals and terrorists differ in their motivations, they should all be regarded as engaging in criminal behavior. However, unlike other criminals, terrorists, particularly terrorist organizations, enjoy claiming credit for the violence that has been perpetrated.

Furthermore, terrorist attacks often go beyond the immediate physical harm they cause, as their victims often experience long-term psychological damage and posttraumatic stress after the terrorist incident. In being able to cause psychological trauma and fear in mass numbers, terrorists are able to publicize their radical ideology, strengthen their cause, generate mass panic, and coerce governments to comply with their demands.

Key Criteria of Terrorism

The use of and reference to key terms can work to facilitate our ability to determine whether the use of counteraction or counter-terrorism policies is justified and required. Governments and agencies refer to these key criteria to determine the core features of terrorism, that is, the target, objective, motive, perpetrator, and legitimacy or legality of the act.

Violence—Walter Laqueur, Center for Strategic and International Studies, states that "the only general characteristic of terrorism generally agreed upon is that terrorism involves violence and the threat of violence." The use of violence by terrorists is simply a piece of the puzzle. It is integrated along with a variety of other tools; however, it defines the very act of terrorism itself. Violence or the threat of it is used as a tool of manipulation and is directly associated with the terrorists' entire motive.

Psychological impact and fear—In this way their attacks are meant to be severe and prolong psychological wounds. Acts of terrorism are considered a performance and created to have a large audience. Terrorists also attack national symbols to show their disregard for their enemy. This also shakes the foundation of the country in question and often the government of that country as well. This increases the legitimacy of the terrorists and often weakens the government's standing in the eyes of its people.

Perpetrated for a political goal—Terrorist attacks usually have a political goal. They are considered in the same vein as protesting; they are created to call attention to a certain situation that the terrorists need addressed. Since the goal of such an operation is the be-all and end-all, no one considers death of civilians a real issue here. This is where terrorism and religion find common ground and work to empower one another. When a terrorist fails on a religious ground, the failure is insurmountable and is worse than the number of civilians who may have died on one of their missions.

Deliberate targeting of noncombatants—It is believed that the goal of terrorism is to target civilians, and that is not untrue as civilians are not targeted because they are threats, but because they are such useful symbols. When those victimized are children, mothers, women, and/or the elderly, it is considered the highest form of criminality and an act against humanity. Terrorists aim to instill extreme fear and moral panic within society, and therefore aim to incur the highest levels of death and suffering to innocent civilians. This also works to attract the eye of the public, an integral part of their game.

Disguise—Among the aims of terrorists is to delegitimize the government in the eyes of the people as an attempt to bring to the surface what they view as wrongful actions being taken by the government, and have the public on their side. One of their techniques is to disguise themselves as civilians and provoke governments into attacking the wrong group, which casts the government in a terrible light. Once the government identifies its enemy, regardless of the measures taken to combat them, "terrorism" is never used to characterize its actions. Mass executions by governments such as the Nazis in World War II are recognized as huge crimes against humanity, but they are rarely referred to as terrorism.

Unlawfulness or illegitimacy—Since it is the government itself that decides what acts belong within the criminal code, that is, defining which acts are *mala prohibita* and which are *mala in se*, it works to legitimize and make lawful any actions it takes, which may otherwise be considered terrorism. For instance, a government may decide to bomb an entire town in the name of providing its citizens with security, freedom, and protection. An example of this was seen when the United States invaded Iraq, or when it bombed rural areas in Pakistan to kill members of the Taliban. Such acts are not masked with terms such as *extremism* or *terrorism*, and are instead replaced with terms such as *patriotism*, *democracy*, and *collateral damage*. This renders concepts such as legitimacy and lawfulness subjective and always in the eyes of the beholder.

1st through 14th Centuries AD

From the Zealots were the Sicario, those who killed Romans for invading their land, Israel.

The Zealots are one of the very first organized groups that resemble modern-day terrorism. They were known to the Romans as "Dagger Men" and rebelled against the Roman Empire, attacking their forces in an underground operation and attacking Jews who worked in association with the Romans as well. The term *Zealot* itself was derived from the Hebrew language and means "one who follows or is an admirer of God." Thus, the justification used for their organization's behaviors and acts of violence was their fundamental belief that they could not be truly faithful to their religion while living under the Roman rule. When the Romans conducted a massive siege leading them close to their capture, the Zealots staged a mass suicide at the Roman fortress of Masada.

The Zealots, who at the time professed a polytheistic religion which was considered pagan, were a faction of the Jewish community that were noted for their extreme opposition to the Romans. The Zealots became an aggressive political party whose goals were focused on maintaining the national and religious lives of the Jewish people. This led the group to even despise members of the Jewish community who sought peace and resolution with the Roman authorities (Encyclopaedia Britannica, 2014).

The next group to be identified as terrorists was the Assassins, known as the Hashashins. Under the leadership of Hasan Al Sabbah, their modus operandi was to directly target and assassinate political leaders, rather than undergo direct combat. The Assassins would be sent out by Hasan, who resided in his hideout located in northern Iran. Since those Assassins would commit suicide upon completion of their mission, this allowed the Assassins to succeed and also provide newly created terrorist groups with their secret to success.

The Zealots and Assassins might only have been operational in antiquity; learning more about them is a possible means for finding answers today. They resemble modern terrorists due to their organization skills and excellent targeting, and more so because they were able to create deep psychological wounds with their actions, as is the case with today's terrorist acts.

14th through 18th Centuries

Toward the end of the Assassins era, which was from the late 13th century to the 1700s, the world saw plenty of barbarism and conflict; however, the acts lacked the needed ingredients to be called terrorism. It was not until the creation of the modern nation with the Treaty of Westphalia in 1648 that terrorism began to rear its head. As communication was understandably inadequate, causes for terrorism were invented and inspired. Such causes included religious schism, insurrection, and ethnic strife. As kingdoms became nations, they became more capable of suppressing violence and terrorism. In fact, the advent of the French Revolution first inspired the words *terrorist* and *terrorism*.

Terrorism as a word was introduced to explain the actions of the revolutionary government in 1795 France. The Committee of Public Safety and the National Convention and their policies were known as terrorists and inspired other states and nations to suppress their citizens with the use of terror. As their only means of maintaining the status quo, their tactics included instilling terror through intimidation and assassinations, along with the implementation of Persian mobs and gangs, which took place during, before, and even after the revolution. Their killing of officials was also instrumental long before the introduction of the guillotine, long noted as the main method of execution during the French Revolution.

Approaching Modern Times: The 19th Century

As technology was enhanced and weapons began to improve in the late 19th century, numerous groups and small factions began to form. Anarchists succeeded in implementing their idea of the "propaganda of the deed" and actually managed to assassinate the heads of state of several nations, including Spain, Russia, and France. They were not, however, organized and had no interest in cooperating with other social movements; thus, their sole intent was the practical element of their idea, rather than the broader symbolic meaning behind the use of violence to target political structures.

At the same time, communism was born as a social movement, but it would not gain momentum until the 20th century. The 19th century also brought forward nationalism, and people who had been oppressed or removed by a new nation began to revolt, leading to well-known struggles, such as Irish nationalism, which till today has not been resolved.

The best-known terrorist group at that time was the Russian Narodnaya Volya (People's Will), led by Andrey I. Zhelyabov and Sofya L. Perovskaya. They were a well-distinguished and distinct Russian organization that was quite different from modern terrorists, as they would call off attacks if they thought they might put civilians in danger, a strategy that may have become extinct with terrorists today. Nonetheless, they very much resembled what we know as terrorism today—which can be seen in their high level of organization, violence, and force used to achieve their goals.

20th-Century Terrorism

Nationalism as an idea began to rise on an international level in the 20th century. During this particular time, national identities became of greater importance to people in different territories. Even though conflicts around nationalism had occurred before, they seemed to escalate at this time.

As people began to stress the importance of relating themselves to certain ethnicities and territories, these ideas became interesting to international political movements. Members of states that had been overtaken by others viewed the concept of nationalism as a cause to support what they believed in and what they thought was theirs. This had an impact on an international level that was not lost to anyone. As with any other movement or ideology, there came about the extremists who resorted to violence and used nationalism as their justification. For instance, the Irish and Macedonian terrorist organizations in Europe used this time to resort to violence and get their causes heard.

Global Terror

The age of modern terrorism commenced when the Popular Front for the Liberation of Palestine (PFLP) hijacked an El Al plane coming from Tel Aviv and going to Rome. Planes had been hijacked before, but this had symbolic value as it had a certain aim. It was also the first time in history where hostages were used to meet demands. This operation gained a lot of attention from the media, which worked to increase both awareness and moral panic.

The head of PFLP, Dr. George Habash, observed that opposed to all the other actions they had periodically taken, finally the world was taking notice. An important note during these times of targeting Muslims is that George Habash was Christian; Palestine was not divided by religious sects, and people fought for Palestine as a nation, not as a religious community.

A newer aspect of the internationalization of terrorists was the sudden cooperation and interaction between extremist organizations. The 1970s saw Palestinians work with radical European groups, as well as the PFLP working with the Japanese Red Army (JRA). These kinds of work relationships continue to this day on an international level.

The division and fighting within Palestine, between the two main rival parties, Fatah and Hamas began when Hamas had taken over the Gaza Strip in 2007. However, they had been meeting for talks and finally came to a joint agreement, which they signed in Egypt during the first week of May 2011. Though this would be viewed as excellent to resolving the clash within Palestine, the Israeli prime minister, Netanyahu, has criticized this agreement and pressured Fatah to cancel it and side with Israel. Though it is noted that the occupation has been accompanied by violence and injustice against Palestine and the Palestinian people, we must also note that Hamas has been classified by the U.S. government and the European Union as a terrorist group.

21st-Century Terrorism

Many might believe that there is a transparent government protocol in existence; besides that, there is still good reason to make use of terrorist profiling as a step forward in promoting greater national security. Despite some controversy in the use of the word *profiling* to identify terrorists, there is good reason to use profiles to target terrorist individuals.

Generally, terrorists fall into one of four categories: psychopathic terrorists, ethnogeographic religious terrorists, ethnogeographic political terrorists, and retributional terrorists. As such, as a category, behaviors and characteristics can be identified in each of these typologies that can help in identifying terrorists.

Terrorists throughout the 19th, 20th, and 21st centuries favored assassinations, bombing, and technology, respectively, as their methods of choice. It is unclear whether past terrorist methods will cease to exist in the future. Regardless, as we continue into a modern technology-governed world, many experts are looking into cyber and ecoterrorism, convinced that they will dominate future terrorist acts. Seemingly, the number of incidents and instances of these, going forward, may increase compared with current incidents.

The world has witnessed a significant increase in terrorist activity, both by nations and by individuals. These attacks took place around the world and with only a day or two in between each event. As already known, certain areas in Afghanistan and Pakistan have remained a hot spot for terrorist activities since the U.S. invasion of Afghanistan, and dating back earlier than that as well. On April 11, 2011, we witnessed what was named the Belarus Blast in Minsk, where a bomb was left beneath a platform and detonated by remote control. The instrument that was utilized aimed to cause the greatest damage; it was indicated that the bomb contained nails and bolts, a common method used by terrorists to ensure that they injure or kill as many as possible. There are a number of theories that have been used to explain this behavior, some saying that it was revenge due to the orders by Lukashenka since there were massive riots against his reelection, and others saying it was planned by foreign terrorists to destabilize their economy and attack their regime. So far, only two suspects have been arrested, and no further information has been released about the matter.

Just days after this tragic event, on April 27, 2011, eight American soldiers were killed at Kandahar Airport by an Afghani suicide bomber who managed to get within the military section of the airport. Another terrorist attack took place on April 28, 2011, bombing the famous Marrakesh Café, killing at least 12 persons. The next day, NATO and the Afghan Army killed 18 Taliban members, termed the "Badr Operation." Of course, the Taliban sent out terrorist threats after the event, threatening to hit back at anyone who sided with NATO or the Afghan Army.

On April 30, 2011, another attack took place in northern Iraq, where seven were killed due to a suicide attack on a checkpoint, and five of those killed were from the Iraqi Army. On May 1, we witnessed another suicide attack by a 12-year-old Afghani child who hit the marketplace, killing four people in Afghanistan.

The next day called for a very significant event for the United States and the world; on May 2, 2011, President Barack Obama declared Osama bin Laden dead, killed during a planned attack by the U.S. Army. While the United States provided

DNA evidence of his death, confirming bin Laden's identity, news channels and papers within the Middle East doubted the validity of the information. However, no pictures were released by the U.S. Pentagon, despite promises to do so for over weeks after his death. This led newspapers such as *Al Ahram* and *Al Yawm Al Saabi'* (both based in Egypt) to argue that his death was fabricated, though they did reiterate the events and procedure involved in the killing as stated by the United States. For instance, Al Khaleej newspapers (based in the United Arab Emirates) stated beneath the picture of bin Laden's alleged villa that it was a Pakistani soldier standing on top of his villa/house that was said to be bin Laden's residence. Countries worldwide increased their levels of security alerts in all tourist destinations and airports.

There were a number of controversies around this event that led officials worldwide to question the validity of the information provided by the U.S. Pentagon and president. It was not until May 9, 2011, that the Taliban admitted to the death of Osama bin Laden, simultaneously having Al Qaeda release an alert for revenge. The first was the so-called Islamic sea burial that the United States had for bin Laden. Several Muslim scholars, such as the Grand Sheikh of Al Azhar (leading world institution for Islamic decisions) in Egypt, condemned this type of burial and confirmed the fact that a sea burial is against Islamic traditions and requirements. The United States argued that its reason for this type of burial was to prevent having bin Laden's burial place become a shrine. Collateral damage was also part of the procedure of killing Osama bin Laden, though this was not highlighted by many officials, where three men and one woman were killed.

Though President Obama did come out after this event and declare that the United States was not at war with Islam, and that bin Laden was in fact not a Muslim leader, the event was interpreted in a number of different ways by different individuals, politicians, and states. For instance, Hamas leader Ismael Haniya and the Muslim Brotherhood of Egypt both condemned the killing of Osama bin Laden, whereas Palestinian Authority spokesman Ghassan Khateeb and Palestinian Prime Minister Salam Fayyad both provided positive feedback from the event, saying that it was a landmark event marking the end of an individual who was involved in terror and destruction.

A release of information by WikiLeaks on May 3, 2011, stating that the United States had known of Osama bin Laden's residence since 2008, led to the rise of a number of comments by different Pakistani authorities. Abu Bakr Al Siddique, a Pakistani writer and political expert, spoke on the Al Jazeera English news channel and confirmed the fact that the Pakistani government was not informed of the attack beforehand. The same confirmation was provided by General Hamid Gul, former director of the Pakistani Inter-Services Intelligence (ISI), saying that the ISI was not aware of the event and that it was viewed as a violation of Pakistani security and sovereignty and an act of war. This view was taken not only by Pakistani officials, but also by former West German Chancellor Helmut Schmidt, who said that it was a clear violation of international law and that the event could have incalculable consequences in the Middle East, Pakistan, and Afghanistan.

On this note, many scholars, political activists, and experts commented on this event, many stating their indifference. For instance, former U.S. intelligence officer Paul Pillar said that as a matter of leadership of terrorist organizations, bin Laden has not been the main story for some time. In fact, it is argued that Osama bin Laden was not the actual leader of Al Qaeda, as the real mentor-leader was Abdullah Azzam. Osama bin Ladin was simply the coordinator.

Paul Pillar also adds that Osama bin Laden is a symbol or source of ideology, but these roles can continue to play out whether he is dead or alive. The same argument is used by Fawaz Gerges, an Al Qaeda expert at the London School of Economics, where he said that bin Laden's death is a significant victory for the United States, but it is more symbolic than concrete and that the world has already moved beyond bin Laden. Another Islamic scholar, Dr. Hani Al Sibaai, also said that bin Laden's death would not change anything and that he was the source of nothing more than an ideology, which does not need to be linked to any organization for that matter. To add to that, Osama bin Laden made a recording of himself after 9/11 stating that his life or death did not matter.

Of course, some will argue, as did a number of newspapers and TV news discourses, that the entire event was coordinated for the sake of President Obama's upcoming elections. On May 3, 2011, just a day after the declaration made by Obama regarding bin Laden's killing, he said the world is now a "better" and "safer" place due to the event. Reuters/Ipsos polls showed that 39% of Americans had an improved view of his presidency and leadership afterward. Yet, the security alerts and threat levels in the United States and U.S. embassies worldwide were increased.

On May 9, 2011, the government of Iran declared that they have strong evidence that Osama bin Laden had died several years ago, and that this whole event was U.S. propaganda. Though this information has not yet been released, nor are we sure that it will be, it only adds to the controversy of the event.

Judging Terrorism

The terms *terrorism* and *terrorist* carry negative connotations, and both refer to something we all think of as very negative. They are often used as labels to refer to the heinousness of a crime. This, of course, furthers the ambiguity connected to terrorism. Viewing the horror of terrorism from a utilitarian's perspective may allow us to justify the act, if the benefits outweigh the costs. Looking at it from a non-utalitarian view, terrorism will never have any moral ground or justification. However, even non-utalitarian philosophers, such as Michael Walzer, have allowed for terrorism to be utilized in extreme measures only, when a community faces extreme threats of complete destruction and this would be their only means of preservation.

There seems to be only two points that everyone agrees on. The first is that the term *terrorism* is attached to negative connotations, and the second is that terrorism is in the eye of the beholder (Hoffman, 2006).

Once a group of individuals successfully applies the label to a certain group, they have successfully persuaded others to view "terrorists" from their own point of view. So when we deem someone a terrorist, it remains clearly subjective and depends on which side we as individuals are on. If we are on the side of the victims, we will easily call it terrorism. If we are on the side of the aggressor, we might call it something else entirely to justify self-defense.

Once again, the certain derogatory connotations can of course be summed up in the quote, "One man's terrorist is another man's freedom fighter." This is true if one group is a friend of the state and initially referred to as "freedom fighter." That very same group, if it falls out of favor, will just as quickly be referred to as "terrorists." This will often be ironically marked by the fact that the group will use methods it has learned while serving under that state to later fight that same state.

The Malayan People's Anti-Japanese Army was labeled "terrorist" by the British during World War II. This was after having been allied with the British government until a fallout occurred and they were designated as their "enemy." In recent years, Ronald Reagan referred to the Afghan Mujahedeen as freedom fighters when he used their resources to fight the Soviets. Twenty years later, that same group was referred to as terrorists by then U.S. President George W. Bush and even later by President Obama.

Terrorism researcher Professor Martin Rudner, director of the Canadian Centre of Intelligence and Security Studies at Ottawa's Carleton University, regards terrorism as any attack against innocent civilians in order to achieve political, religious, or ideological goals. Rudner also believes that the famous statement "One man's terrorist is another man's freedom fighter" is invalid and focuses solely on end results of the acts, thus using the goal to justify the means, when terrorism is never a justifiable means.

Western media tends to adopt a very narrow categorization system in their means of identifying who is a terrorist versus who is a statesman, usually focusing solely on their measure of success. Excellent illustrations of this include the Nobel Peace Prize laureates Menachem Begin and Nelson Mandela.

There are also incidents of states that have been close allies for generations suddenly disagreeing on whether members of certain organizations are terrorists. For many years, the U.S. government did not consider the Irish Republican Army (IRA) as terrorists, even when they were using terrorist methods against the British, a strong U.S. ally.

Even though the terms *terrorism* and *extremism* are sometimes used in the same sentence or even interchangeably, there remains a significant difference between them. Terrorism is a call to and threat of violence. Extremism is about achieving a political goal and changing minds to fit one's own agenda. Al Qaeda engaged in terrorism, and the Iranian revolution was about extremism. Media outlets that want to remain impartial are extremely careful about how they use the terms. However, a report by the Strategic Foresight Group (2007) estimates that extremism will be more of a threat than terrorism in the years to come. The objectives of extremist groups focus largely on infiltrating their ideas into the minds of individuals, especially youth. Extremists are no longer engaging in terrorist acts but are instead aiming to and promising the people of reaching a "better world." The term *better*, of course, is relative, since it originates from their own perspective. Their strategy has been proven successful in several countries. For example, the Muslim Brotherhood in Egypt won a large percentage of Parliament seats in the elections of 2005. Likewise, the theocratic regime in Iran has currently grown and become more powerful and influential.

Since extremism tends to act as a precursor to terrorism, the main issue is how those extremists enforce their beliefs. If a violent means is taken, then those extremists have now become terrorists (Martin, 2009). This smooth dispersion of extremist groups and their success across a number of countries is viewed by many as a dangerous phenomenon facing the coming generations.

Participants of Terrorism

Terrorism can be the act of an individual, state, nation, or group. Some terrorists are state sponsored and carry out their actions in the peripheries of certain nations and outside a legitimate war. The deadliest operations have been those set up and carried out by small factions with a political and religious cause, much like the terrorists that carried out the attacks on 9/11, the London Underground, and the 2002 Bali bombing. These were groups who organized their attacks on a smaller level, relying on close-knit circuits of friends and family, and the easily accessible public information as there was a minimum of speculation about them. They were hidden from the eyes of law enforcement agencies and national security. They also used technologies to their benefit, using cell phones and computers to an advanced degree as the basis of their entire plan (Reid et al., 2004). Ever since the commencement of such attacks, some scholars have tried, over the years, to come up with a simple profile for such terrorists. Some, however, like Roderick Hindery, have chosen to study their modus operandi rather than carrying out studies of their personalities.

State Sponsors

Certain nations have been known to sponsor terrorists by either funding or hiding operating organizations. There are many arguments for and against whether state-sponsored terrorism is actually terrorism and numerous accusations made against a large number of countries. However, when states fund certain groups, it's usually in a very secretive manner and is not disclosed to the public.

State Terrorism

Needless to say, even mentioning that there is such a thing as state-sponsored terrorism is quite controversial. We know that military actions, even when the civilian head count is high, do not constitute as terrorism, even if some methods are the same. State terrorism is simply not an international legal concept, even though the chairman of the United Nations Counter-Terrorism Committee has stated that there are 12 international conventions on the subject. If a nation abuses not only its power but also its laws, it should be held responsible under the international conventions that pertain to war crimes, international human rights, and international humanitarian law.

Kofi Annan, former United Nations secretary general, does not support the concepts of state terrorism and believes that the use of force by any state is already regulated by international law. He also argues that defining *terrorism* is not required, but rather that any planned attack on civilians should constitute a crime and be penalized by the law.

Since the term *state terrorism* is used to explain terrorist acts performed by governmental agents or forces, these include any resources used by the state, such as foreign policies and/or military action, to forcefully bring about its goals. According to Michael Stohl (1984), this includes events such as Germany's bombing of London and the U.S. atomic destruction of Hiroshima. It is also evident that the use of state terrorism is more common within the international realm than by insurgents. Look at state means of enforcing terrorism, such as the "first strike," which allows one state to engage in a preemptive unforeseen attack using massive force against another state in order to render the opposing side incapable of counterattacking. Such acts are referred to as a means of crisis management rather than terrorism.

It has been argued that state terrorism as foreign policy was born after World War II. It is believed that the birth of weapons of mass destruction and increasing violent behavior have become somewhat more tolerable (Stohl, 1984). This is also known to be directly correlated to the increased state of moral panic that is widespread and specifically exaggerated in North America and Europe. Their governments have increased the people's state of constant fear, initially declaring terrorists, aka the "enemy," from without, and then declaring them to be within as well. Such a declaration functioned to increase hostility, fear, and discrimination. Combined with special emphasis on stereotypes, this terrorized the public and pressured them into giving up their literal and ideological rights and freedoms. This indirectly permitted state and international terrorism to take place.

This was clearly illustrated after 9/11, when the U.S. government took extreme measures of security, raised the level of threat to the country, and alerted their people to increase fear since the enemy was no longer outside America, but in fact within America itself. This allowed them to create the Patriot Act, increase security measures, and include more invasive and surveillance schemes to "keep an eye" on the people. Many supported these efforts and easily gave up their rights for the sake of security. However, as time passed, many pushed to bring back the balance between security and individual rights.

Another example of such circumstances is the bombing of Pan Am Flight 103. This event received so much attention by the media and was eventually named the Lockerbie bombing. It was immediately characterized as terrorism due to the fact that members of the U.S. intelligence and security services were killed, hence giving rise to a number of conspiracy theories. Claims that a number of European countries were provided with a warning from the Palestinian Liberation Organization (PLO) that extremists would be taking such an action, along with claims from the Central Intelligence Agency (CIA) that the Islamic Jihad Organization had planted the bomb, as well as an alleged confirmation that Libya was responsible for the act, all functioned to terrorize the West, making them more tolerant to any form of counteraction by their governments, which even they themselves would characterize as terrorists (Elliot & Sapsted, 1988).

Studies failed to take into account the imperfections of democracies and Western liberalism (Rummel, 1997). Evidence does in fact show that the more freedom people have, the less the violence there is; however, acts of violence imposed on foreign countries by democratic countries that cause mass murders and democide must also be taken into account. For instance, the indiscriminate bombing of the Vietnamese population by the United States accounts for thousands of civilian fatalities, and that was only one of their foreign attacks (Rummel, 1994). Democide not only is explained by the level of democracy, but also includes the extent to which a country is involved in external wars (Rummel, 1995). Therefore, if all results are combined, we can conclude that democracies enjoy minimal internal violence; however, there is a general trend that they are involved in foreign democide. Regardless of their overall motive and goal, this can be seen in the United States, Canadian, and other Western armies currently within Afghanistan today.

Factors That May Contribute to Terrorism

There are a wide range of factors that play a role in leading individuals toward terrorist organizations, or even engaging in terrorist acts alone. Some believe that terrorism pertains to socioeconomic issues, while others believe that political factors are significant in the formation of terrorist groups. However, collectively, the following factors can be considered key in contributing to the growth of terrorism.

- Poverty
- High population growth rates
- High unemployment
- Environmental problems with the land
- Lagging economics
- Political disenfranchisement

- Extremism
- Ethnic conflict
- Religious conflict
- Territorial conflict

It becomes especially difficult to identify motives when the attack is carried out on a large scale and is unclaimed by any group or individual. This in-turn causes further damage to society and may cause mass hysteria and panic. When it's done on a large scale and remains completely unrelated to any conflict, like the sarin gas attack on the Tokyo subway by Aum Shinrikyo, where no group or individual has claimed responsibility, it becomes even more disturbing and causes more damage to populations. The group of international researchers who put together the report previously cited (Strategic Foresight Group, 2007) took a closer look at terrorism as we know it today. They view terrorism much in the way we view the economic market: greed and upsets create the need for terrorism; supply is driven by deficits, whether they happen to be developmental or democratic deficits.

Terrorist acts occur at the crossroads where supply and demand meet. Those with a demand access the tools of religion, politics, or some ideology to create a working relationship with those supplying terrorism. This is a clear and popular pattern and has been observed from Colombia to Colombo and the Philippines to Palestine.

The Effect of Mass Media

There is a possibility that media exposure is a huge goal of terrorists. As earlier stated, terrorists want to impress their beliefs as well as impose their extremist ideology on others. Therefore, the media is of high value to terrorist organizations, as it allows them to expose their ideologies to the world on a large scale and instill fear in others of their progress. When a terrorist attack occurs, it is often noted that news networks spend extensive hours covering the attack, often shining a spotlight on the terrorist group. In doing so, terrorists are able to gain audiences, often at national and international levels, to watch and feel terrorized by their acts.

With regard to media coverage of terrorist attacks, some experts feel that terrorists have successfully exploited media outlets to their advantage. They believe that the media has given terrorist organizations a voice and that terrorism is almost a symptom, and somewhat of a brainchild, of the media. Paul Watson, a wildlife environmentalist and activist, thinks that the media is somewhat responsible for the increasing number of terrorists and terror attacks, and states that the terrorists use the media as their sole means of delivering information to the public. Interestingly, Paul Watson's organization, Sea Shepherd, a vessel that is involved in direct action taken against whaling ships, and attempts to sabotage them, has been labeled an ecoterrorist organization. However, the organization has not yet claimed any casualties.

In an era of social media, where information is spread at a rapid pace, it is easy for terrorists to recruit members through various social media groups, such as Facebook and Twitter, as well as spread propaganda material. As such, organizations such as the Islamic State of Iraq and the Levant (ISIL) have recruited many of their members from the United States and Europe by spreading their ideology on online forums and social media groups. In addition, ISIL terrorists have utilized social media as a tool to spread videos of beheadings of their prisoners as a way send threats to governments of Western democratic countries, as well as to spread fear in the millions of people around the world who watch them.

Though there have been efforts made by the media to censor certain people or organizations that carry out terrorism in hopes of prevention, this may in fact act to further exasperate the situation and cause unheard of or suppressed terrorists to become more violent to attract the attention they desire. The Weather Underground is a good example of how an organization, while causing no casualties, did not get any media attention until they succumbed to using terrorist acts. As of today, the media remains the largest outlet for terrorism.

The Success and Failure of Counter-Terrorism

There are many known ways in which governments and authorities respond to terrorism. Some choose to look at possible fractures within the political spectrum and even fractures in the fundamental values of a nation, state, or people, in an effort to amend them. Certain responses to terrorism, often called counter-terrorism, generally have a narrow purpose and rely on extensive research and information about terrorists in action. Counter-terrorism responses include arresting individuals who have engaged in terrorist activity, or have future plans to do so, usually through specific criminal proceedings for terror-related crimes. Counter-terrorism measures would also include detaining individuals and engaging in interrogative techniques to seek out additional information or deporting individuals who have conspired in terror activities. Other counter-terrorism measures include surveillance of targeted individuals within the community through public cameras, telephone conversations, or monitoring their Internet activity.

Unfortunately, while these counter-terrorism measures have been put in place, the manner in which they are implemented can lead to problems within counter-terrorism efforts. It is noted that a number of counter-terrorist behaviors adopted by governments do in fact infringe upon human rights and weaken the entire democratic infrastructure. These infringements are fought against by many citizens in democratic nations in Europe, as well as in Canada and the United States. However, they are greatly outnumbered by a large portion of the population that react to the state-induced fear and allow, possibly even request, their governments to take such extreme measures to guarantee the protection and security of their people. Although security has dramatically increased over the years, there seems to be no decrease in the number of terrorist acts taking place. Therefore, it is recommended that these governments consider counter-terrorism measures that tackle the causes of the acts rather than the acts themselves. Newer counter-terrorism strategies and methods are discussed in Chapter 10, which focuses on eradicating the terrorist ideology, instead of fighting against terrorists themselves.

For this publication, the definition of *terrorism* is simplified:

> *Terrorism is a deliberate method of warfare*
> *in which random or symbolic victims*
> *become targets of violence.*

Chapter 2

Analysis with Psychological Defense Styles

Psychologists at times tend to see political and/or religious goals as an arena in which emotions, originating outside those realms, are stimulated and played out. So, a psychologist may ask, what nonpolitical frustrations or drives are at the base of such behavior? Berkowitz (1969) points out two basic variations on this theme. The first stresses the situation in which an individual suffers from the negative effects of previous negative events, such as a social or emotional frustration, or the death of a loved one. This situation is the foundation that allows the development of an internal inclination to become more violent and aggressive. This is especially exaggerated when combined with a political trigger or stimulation.

Berkowitz's (1975) second variation is that an individual may be preconditionally aroused or excited without any aggression and under appropriate conditions. When an alternative and functional outlet for expression is not available, this excitement may be channeled into political violence. This can be seen in a classic example of an organization that starts off initially having no motive or agenda and then suddenly transforms into one that carries characteristics similar to a violent mob.

Berkowitz's ideas seem to resonate with the general aggression model (GAM) (Anderson & Bushman, 2002), which can be used to understand why terrorists do violent things. For violence to occur, there needs to be the presence of two input variables: situational and individual. For a terrorist to carry out a violent act, situation variables such as weapons, terrorist motivators and leaders, and frustration-inducing stimuli must be present. Individual variables such as biological hormones, personality factors, and an inclination toward violence interact with these situational input variables to produce cognitive, emotional, and physiological effects. This process leads to automatic appraisal, and the terrorist may see the target as hostile, provocative, and deserving of punishment. Automatic appraisals lead to reappraisals, which is when the terrorist makes a conscious effort to see the target as the enemy. These reappraisals become unconscious over time, and any seemingly threatening stimuli is seen as a target for the terrorist's violence.

To better understand a terrorist's world, one should take a look at the childhood of a terrorist. It is interesting to note that almost all terrorists come from abusive and dysfunctional families (DeMause, 2004; Gallimore, 2004). Individuals who grow up to join terrorist organizations or become violent offenders often have troubled pasts fueled with instances of emotional, verbal, physical, and sexual abuse (Craparo, Schimmenti, & Caretti, 2013). These experiences cause trauma, leading to rage, hostility, and antisocial tendencies when unresolved (Gallimore, 2004).

According to the social cognitive theory (SCT) by Albert Bandura (1986), individuals acquire information and behaviors by observing models, who are people the learners look up to and whose behaviors the learners emulate. In a terrorist's world, these models are often charismatic and convincing trainers recruited to produce a future generation of terrorists (Khelgat-Doost, 2017). The SCT also states that the learner must be attentive to and retain the information, as well as be motivated to learn it. Finally, successful learning takes place when the learner is able to emulate and practice the learned behaviors (Bandura, 1977). Terrorist training camps provide an environment where these conditions are met. Moreover, positive reinforcement by the trainers in the form of praise and financial and social benefits serves as increased motivation for the learning of extremist behaviors, ideologies, and values.

Terrorism: A Psychoanalytical Perspective

Terrorists claim to commit violent crimes due to political, religious, and economic motives. It is possible that these may just be superficial reasons that are used to hide a deep-seated psychoanalytical conflict within the mind of a terrorist. These unconscious conflicts emerge during childhood and are often a result of negligent parenting and incidents of traumatic abuse (Stein, 2006). Negligent and dismissive parenting results in the child's failure to develop a sense of self as well as diminished self-confidence (Brown & Murphy, 2011). It also leads to the feeling of being invisible, which may eventually lead to bursts of excitement and violence to achieve recognition. This is evident in the acts of criminals, violent offenders, and terrorists, who strive to gain respect from the enemy, as well as be recognized worldwide (Gilligan, 2003). Hence, they may cherish the recognition and enjoy terrorizing nations as it enhances their low self-esteem. This may be why there is a surge in terrorist attacks following media coverage of a previous attack (Jetter, 2017).

A factor that stands out in many terrorist case profiles is the absence of a father during the terrorist's childhood. It may also be that the father is present but is highly dismissive, emotionally unavailable, and physically abusive. The mother is often a woman with a weak personality, unable to bridge the gap between the father and child, and often resorts to being abusive herself. This results in the child developing an avoidant attachment style characterized by mistrust, wariness of caregivers and strangers, and suppression of desires of emotional warmth or affection (Renken et al., 1989). Lacking an attachment figure to rely on in times of distress, the child turns toward an alternate figure. In the terrorist's case, this attachment figure is often a religious leader or God himself (Varvin & Volkan, 2003). A history of traumatic abuse also leads to self-victimization.

Research conducted by Jeanne Knutson in 1981 allowed her to argue that victimization remains the motivating force behind much political violence in the contemporary world. Victimization is defined as a personally experienced injustice, which the victim recognizes to be unnecessary (or unjust), and which creates a basic fear of annihilation. Discrete events that may cause victimization and have the strength to change the victim's perception of the world can cause them to defend themselves or their group in order to reduce the chances of experiencing secondary victimization against the self, family, community, or all three. Since a majority of terrorist activity will involve some form of victimization, we recognize a vicious cycle where terrorism and victimization breed and feed into one another.

Over the span of his career, the author had the opportunity to study and get to know a number of terrorists and violent offenders, several of whom he went on to later formally interview and generate data for research.

As an assessment tool to assist in profiling analysis, the author utilized the Defense Style Questionnaire (DSQ) (Bond, 1992). Using this scale, defense styles were presented to the accused in the form of statements or questions that were to be rated on a scale of 1 to 9. The data gathering began with an initial structured interview and questionnaire administration. During the interviews, individuals began describing their life in general at first, then thoughtfully moving on to family dynamics, goals and expectations, desires, fears, and dreams.

An unstructured and informal discussion volunteered by the accused followed the interview, all of which was later reported to have felt cathartic for the accused.

The documented interviews and data were analyzed and interpreted. There were five statistical columns present:

1. N is the number of participants that responded to the particular question.
2. Minimum: Refers to the lowest number chosen by a participant on the Likert scale response format for each question.
3. Maximum: Refers to the highest number chosen by a participant on the Likert scale response format for each question.
4. Mean: The average of all responses.
5. Standard deviation: Provides an index of variability concerning the distribution of scores.

It is interesting to note that of all 88 statements analyzed, statement 44, "I would rather win than lose in a game," had the highest mean among the participants.

Mean = 8.92
Standard deviation = 0.277
Minimum = 8
Maximum = 9

It can be seen that the standard deviation (0.227) of all responses for this statement is low, indicating that all participants had similar responses. In fact, the detailed frequency showed that 92.3% of the participants circled the number 9 for the question, which means that they strongly agreed with the statement "I would rather win than lose in a game."

In contrast, statement 79, "I take drugs, medicine, or alcohol when I'm tense," had the lowest mean score.

Mean = 1.08
Standard deviation = 0.277
Minimum = 1
Maximum = 2

With a similarly low standard deviation, it can be assumed that all responses were fairly homogenous, and hence most accused terrorists did not resort to drugs, medicine, or alcohol when stressed or tense.

Descriptive statistics were generated to give insight into the demographics of the accused terrorists, including those of educational level, age, nationality, and marital status.

The majority of the participants (53.8%) belong to the age group of 22–35 year olds, followed by 38.5% in the 36–50 year old group and 7.7% in the 19–21 year old group. Analysis revealed that most of the accused (53.8%) were aged between 22 and 35. Interestingly, only 7.7% of the participants were young adults aged between 19 and 21, while 38.5% of the participants were older adults between the ages of 36 and 50. This comes as a mild surprise. One would associate committing terror activities with impulsivity and assume that younger adults would be more influenced to take part.

This suggests that in the case of these participants, joining a terrorist organization may not have been a result of an impulsive choice, but instead a well-thought-out decision taking years to formulate.

With regard to their educational background, findings suggest that the majority of participants have received some formal education, with 38.5% holding bachelor's degrees and 23.1% having received high school diplomas.

Most participants were reported to have been married (46.2%), while 38.5% admitted to being single and 7.7% divorced. Unsurprisingly, many of them were parents to between one and five children. One surprising finding was that a vast majority of the participants reported to having suffered a serious traumatic event in their life. This seemed to have been a common theme across many responders, who admitted to having been deeply impacted by this incident. It is also worth mentioning that though most participants had traumatic backgrounds, none reported that they are or have been affiliated with a particular terror cell. This item remained blank on all response sheets of the DSQ. As professions, these people involved themselves in a number of trades, mainly belonging to lower-tier or subordinate jobs, such as car mechanics, carpenters, or taxi drivers.

Through the data generated, a clear picture of the accused begins to emerge. It should be noted that this picture may not be applicable to all terrorists and violent offenders, but instead is a representation of the average terrorist encountered by the author during his research. The average terrorist seems to be a young adult male aged 28, married, with one child. He has some formal education and has at least received a high school diploma. This individual has experienced significant trauma in his life, which has deeply impacted his personality and outlook toward the world. This trauma may be partly responsible for him carrying out terrorist activities. However, when questioned on whether he is affiliated with a terrorist cell, he refrains from delving into any information. As a profession, he works in a low-tier job and may be a handyman, carpenter, or taxi driver. Though he does not earn much, this individual is very competitive and strives to win at everything, which supposedly enhances his self-worth. When under stress, he does not resort to alcohol, medication, or drugs, but instead may rely on religious activities to relieve his stress.

Relationship between Demographic Factors and Defense Styles

The demographic portion had several aspects: age group, education level, marital status, number of children, trauma experienced, affiliation with a terror cell, and professional skills.

Age group: 53.8% of the participants in the sample belong to the age group 22–35 year olds, followed by 38.5% in the 36–50 year old group and 7.7% in the 19–21 year old group.

Educational level: The highest degree obtained by the participants in the following sample is a bachelor's degree. 38.5% of the participants appear to have obtained a bachelor's degree. The same amount of participants noted that they have not acquired any degree. Last, 23.1% of the participants obtained high school degrees.

Marital status: 46.2% of the participants are married, while 38.5% are single and 7.7% are divorced. There is one missing value with this question. A small number of participants would not answer it.

Number of children: 53.8% of the participants have between zero and two children, while 38.5% of the participants have between three and five children. A small number of participants would not answer this question.

Trauma experienced: 84.6% of the participants noted having experienced a trauma, while 15.4% didn't note any particular traumatic event. This subsection noted how many participants completed the "trauma experienced" inquiry. It did not ask about the kind of trauma but did ask about any experience with traumatic events in their lives.

Affiliation with a terror cell: It is worth mentioning that none of the participants reported that they were affiliated to a particular terror cell. This remained blank on all of the answer sheets.

Professional skills: There was a wide range of answers in the professional skills section. Many of the professional skills mentioned fall under the category of lower-tier or subordinate jobs, such as car mechanic, carpenter, taxi driver, and "worked in an apiary." The rest fall under the umbrella of business or business owner (e.g., owner of a restaurant).

The Spearman's rho, a nonparametric test used to measure the strength of association between two variables, was used for statistical measures. Correlations were significant at the 0.01 level (two-tailed). The reported results indicate only the factors that show a correlation.

The defense styles presented were maladaptive, image distorting, self-sacrificing, adaptive, neurotic denial, nondelusional projection, passive-aggression, acting out, splitting of other's image, projective identification, omnipotence, undoing, affiliation, somatization, hypochondriasis, pseudoaltruism, passive-aggression, suppression, projection, sublimation, lie, humor, regression, inhibition, reaction formation, denial, devaluation, withdrawal, fantasy, splitting, primitive idealization, anticipation, help-rejecting complaining, isolation, consumption, task orientation, and isolation strong.

A significant relationship was found between the acting-out defense style and the education level of the participant, with a negative correlation of -0.615, significant at $p < 0.05$. This means that the more an individual is educated, the more likely they are to disagree with the questions measuring acting out.

Significant relationship was found between the somatization defense style and the education level of the participant, with a negative correlation of -0.589, significant at $p < 0.05$. This may mean that the higher an individual's education exposure, the less likely they may be to admit to the questions measuring somatization.

Similarly, a significant relationship was found between the hypochondriasis defense style and the education level of the participant, with a negative correlation of -0.593, significant at $p < 0.05$. This may mean that the more educated an individual is, the less likely they are to admit to the questions measuring hypochondriasis.

A significant association was found between the projection defense style and the education level of the participants, with a negative relationship (-0.800, $p < 0.01$), suggesting that individuals with higher education levels are less prone to using projection as a defense mechanism.

Analysis unraveled two significant relationships associated with the lie defense style: (1) a negative correlation with age group (-0.601, $p < 0.05$), meaning that the older the individual, the more likely that they will be to disagree with the statements of the lie defense style; and (2) a negative correlation with the number of children (-0.613, $p < 0.05$), meaning that the more children the individual has, the more likely that they will be to disagree with the statements of the lie defense style.

A significant relationship was found between the reaction formation defense style and trauma experienced by the individuals, with a positive correlation (0.575, $p < 0.05$), indicating that individuals who have experienced trauma are more likely to agree with the statements of the reaction formation defense style.

A significant relationship was found between the help-rejecting complaining defense style and educational level, with a negative correlation (-0.733, $p < 0.05$), indicating that the higher the person's level of education, the more likely this person is to disagree on the statements of this defense style.

The above correlation table indicates that there are significant correlations when analyzing the questions pertaining to the self-sacrificing defense style, along with the education level of the participants.

Education level is negatively correlated with measuring self-sacrificing: "I get satisfied from helping others and if this were taken away from me I would get depressed." The correlation coefficient of -0.590, significant at $p < 0.05$, indicates that the higher the person's education, the less likely they are to disagree with this statement.

Questions positively correlated while measuring the same defense style were

"I tend to ignore unpleasant facts as if they didn't exist."
"I believe in turning the other cheek when someone hurts me."
"If someone mugged me and stole my money, I'd rather he'd be helped than punished."
"My philosophy is hear no evil, do no evil, see no evil."

While a relationship between personal factors and defense styles may seem unusual at first, research findings suggest that a person's demographic factors increase or decrease the likelihood for the use of certain defense styles. One such factor is the education level of a person. Results show that this factor is negatively correlated with a number of defense styles, including acting out, somatization, hypochondriasis, pseudoaltruism, projection, and help-rejecting complaining. In simpler terms, this indicates that the higher a person's educational qualification is, the lower is the likelihood of them using these defense styles. For instance, a highly educated person is less likely to use projection as a defense mechanism than someone with a lower educational qualification. In contrast, education level was positively correlated with the defense mechanism of self-sacrificing, suggesting that those with higher educational qualifications are more likely to perform self-sacrificing behaviors than individuals with fewer educational qualifications.

The age group of a person was also seen to influence the likelihood of them using certain defense styles. Age group was positively correlated with pseudoaltruism, while being negatively correlated with lying. This suggests that as the individual gets older, they are more likely to engage in altruistic behaviors for personal gain, while decreasing their lying behaviors. Similarly, pseudoaltruism was seen to be positively correlated with marital status, suggesting that married or divorced individuals were more likely to engage in these behaviors than single participants. It was also observed that participants who were currently married or had been in the past did not engage in passive aggression as much as those who were single.

The presence of children also had an influence on the use of certain defense styles. Findings suggested that pseudoaltruism increased and the use of lying decreased with an increase in the number of children. Another finding that was deemed important by the author was the correlation between reaction formation and the factor of trauma experienced by the participants. Findings suggested that participants experiencing traumatic incidents in life are more likely to use reaction formation than those who have not encountered significant traumatic events.

Hence, these participants may express their deep-seated impulses in contrasting and opposite behaviors as a form of coping with their past trauma.

An analysis of these findings highlights the key role of the education level as a factor of significant correlations with defense styles. Hence, the education level of a participant may reveal elaborate insights upon further research and may help us understand the role of education level in terrorism.

In summary, the last part of the statistical analysis revealed correlations between defense styles and demographics. The following defense styles are the one who were strongly associated with specific demographics: help-rejecting complaining, reaction formation, lie, projection, passive-aggression, pseudoaltruism, hypochondriasis, somatization, and acting out.

Interestingly, most of these defense styles were shown to be associated with the education level, which suggests that a prospective study investigating education level and defense styles more closely would be interesting.

Chapter 3

Types of Terrorists

In 1986, an invitation was extended to me by Dr. Edward Azar to join the University of Maryland, Center for International Development and Conflict Management (CID/CM) as a 1986 visiting fellow. The attracting interest from the director was a peer-reviewed article on cultural sects in the Levant region. Interest diverted to the study of the psychology of terrorism, but more specifically the psychology of terrorists: fundamentalism and hostage situations. This fellowship resulted in a national conference sponsored by the CID/CM, the Spouses of Diplomats Auxiliary, and the Center for Victims of Trauma.

As research began in this think tank center, several influences arose. The conflict in the Middle East produced a continued supply of terrorist groups. The world became focused on this Arab region more than other locations. Many people believed that all Arabs are Muslim, not knowing that there are Jewish Arabs, Christian Arabs, and Muslim Arabs. It was apparently easier to label everyone in a small categorical box as Arab Muslims. Public opinion via media and political propaganda machines was glad to see terrorism as the inhumane vehicle of Arabs who just happened to be Muslim.

Training in clinical psychology teaches each student and supervises each intern to be open to all possibilities. Psychology imparts strategies to assist the professional to not takes sides but seek the truth. It uses standardized instruments to measure intelligence, emotions, behavior, and neuropsychology, to move away from wrongful accusation in pursuit of those who actually committed the crime of terrorism. It is too easy to blame anyone based on skin color, religion, nationality, or creed—the premorbid factors that lead to racial prejudice and support bias development.

Types of terrorism was a growing industry for political scientists and behavioral scientists during the 1970s and 1980s. Many scholars in the military and private groups gained momentum seeking definition and strategies for terrorism and counter-terrorism. As in any process, the work is ongoing and may never end. There is always more to learn with each encounter. The knowledge gained in one episode will help us to know more about the next situation that could come.

In 1975, the National Advisory Committee on Criminal Justice Standards and Goals was formed by the Law Enforcement Assistant Administration in the United States. A volume was produced by the task force on disorders and terrorism; it classifies terrorism into six identifiable categories: civil disorders, political terrorism, nonpolitical terrorism, quasi-terrorism, limited political terrorism, and official or state terrorism (aka structural terrorism).

In the last decade, two more types of terrorism were added to the list above as submitted by Alex Schmid and Albert Jongman (2005): international terrorism and transitional terrorism.

The occurrences happening in the Middle East and world today all serve as examples of the types of terrorism stated above. Newspapers and news channels within the Middle East and elsewhere, such as *Al Bayan* (Dubai, United Arab Emirates), Al Masry Al Yawm (Cairo, Egypt), Al Jazeera (Doha, Qatar), BBC (UK), and the *Washington Times* (United States), are documenting what can be defined as terrorism taking place against the people. Official or state terrorism took place during the Tunisian and Egyptian revolutions, and is currently taking place within Syria, Yemen, Libya, and Bahrain, which are using their military forces to suppress opposition riots and protesters who are demanding political change, using weapons, tear gas, and threats to bring about their silence.

Another act that can be characterized as state terrorism took place when the U.S. government claimed to have killed the all-famous terrorist Osama bin Laden, on May 2, 2011 (Al Jazeera & Al Shorooq). The United States engaged in a raid on his home in Abbottabad, Pakistan, that led to his death and the death of three other civilians, an act that General Hamid Gul, former director of the Pakistani Inter-Services Intelligence (ISI), characterized as a violation of their sovereignty and security and an act of war against Pakistan (Al Jazeera, May 3, 2011).

In 1999, U.S. intelligence analysis (Hudson) found four typologies for terrorists: nationalist-separatist, religious fundamentalist, new religious, and social revolutionary. This will be briefly explained below and a more detailed analysis will be made in the chapters to come.

Many others were instrumental in researching, qualifying, and maybe quantifying their findings. And everyone was correct based on the information they had collected from the individuals they had met to interview or interrogate.

Rather than competition for "who knows the most" or who should be "recognized as the most," the collaboration of information between those who shared their findings resulted in the enhancement of awareness and acceptance of assessment from which there was a gain—a new interpretation of motive, confirmation of material already learned, detection of deliberate lies and misleading information, and more reason to cooperate and not compete.

With language usage ability, although not fluent, information was best understood since the context of the words was part of the interpretative analysis and not just words translated. Translating word for word does not allow a full understanding of the content. Interpretation allows the content to be accommodated and assimilated for cultural correctness in word usage.

With the research on terrorism, more than terrorists themselves, and direct profiling of the accused individuals, there seemed to be preference to categorize into four parts: psychopathic, ethnogeographic—political, ethnogeographic—religious, and retributional (Figure 3.1).

Psychopathic terrorist: An individual who is hired to kill or harm, or to threaten to kill or harm, people for a terrorist group or terrorist state. This person may not know the purpose and may not care to know. They are narcissistically engaged, which complements their psychological personality disorder. They show little or no moral and ethical understanding and demonstrate no remorse of illegal and inhuman actions against others.

Ethnogeographic—religious terrorist: This individual has a cause—to uphold a particular spiritual belief or system that shares the same or similar belief of eternal righteous salvation. And whoever believes in the same, dies for the same (volunteer or hostage), or both, will gain everlasting rewards.

Ethnogeographic—political terrorist: This individual has a cause—to uphold a particular nationalistic or global socioeconomic decree or system that shares the same or similar ruling of righteous security for a country or the world. And whoever believes in the same, dies for the same (volunteer or hostage), or both will gain notoriety in history for making a better place for people to life.

Retributional terrorist: This individual seeks revenge against the person, group, or nation that took away their family, community, or personal way of life.

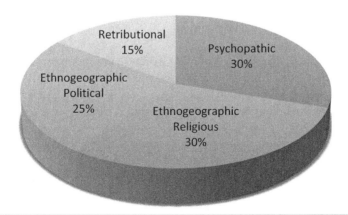

Figure 3.1   Categories by percentage of accused individuals assessed. The percentage breakdown of the four types of terrorists is as follows: 30% psychopathic; 25% ethnogeographic–political, 30% ethnogeographic–religious, and 15% retributional.

Their respective history shows no indication of psychological disorder, and they do not adhere to any political or religious ideology.

These four types of terrorists are discussed further in the next three chapters.

Note that the terminology is interchangeable. *Antisocial personality disorder* is a clinical term, while the term *psychopath* is the forensic word choice. By clinical definition, psychopathology is any mental disorder, but in forensics the same word is perceived as antisocial or narcissistic personality disorder.

During the year long study there, it was recognized that not all terrorists are psychopathic or had any extremist conditioning at home or in their environment, but they may have suffered significant loss, politically driving them to acts of unwarranted and unjustified violence. These are retributional terrorists, only seeking to strike the designated perpetrator who took away loved ones by murder (direct or bystander) and/or destroyed the physical community, job potential, education opportunities, and freedom of human rights.

Neuropsychological explanations are applicable for some. For those who are diagnosed as having antisocial personality disorder, it is possible that tumors in brain areas provoke aggression and negative characteristics.

What may be evident is the brain plasticity during or following a critical event, and certainly probable earlier in the planning stages of a terror act. But this would be premorbid or likely to show on a functional magnetic resonance imaging (fMRI), which measures brain activity by detecting changes associated with blood flow (European Magnetic Resonance Forum, 2014). This technique relies on the fact that cerebral blood flow and neuronal activation are coupled. When an area of the brain is in use, blood flow to that region also increases (Logothetis, 2001).

Neuroplasticity—or brain plasticity—is the ability of the brain to modify its connections or rewire itself (http://theconversation.com/what-is-brain-plasticity-and-why-is-it-so-important-55967). As understood, every thought, feeling, behavior, and intervention (audio, visual) will influence these changes in the brain wiring.

Therefore, such investigations of brain structure may not be reliable as an indicator of terrorism or terrorist character, although the measure is valid. The instrument does measure brain activity, but the total analysis may not be applicable for ethnogeographic religious or political and retributional terrorists.

There is research showing that people of conservative and liberal attribution are different in personality preferences. Yet these virtues don't constitute labeling as terrorist.

Also presumed was that the leaders of terror cells have attributes of narcissistic entitlement syndrome (NES). Upon analyzing all the psychological facts involved with the different types of terrorists, we found that there is one characteristic that is consistent. Individuals who choose terrorism as a means to declare their loathing of this world demonstrate the characteristic of narcissism.

Narcissism is a personality trait that involves egotism and selfishness, and if it is applied to a group, it can also involve elitism or indifference to others. The term was originally coined by Ovid, a Greek poet, who narrated a story of an individual named Narcissus who fell in love with his own reflection. Though a healthy amount of self-love is required to develop in a psychologically healthy way, narcissism is an extreme measure of self-love.

When a person joins a group similar to a cult, they tend to take extreme measures to become one of them and lose the balance between themselves and others, reaching a sense of loss of identity.

A major understanding of members of terrorist cells is NES. Terrorists who experience NES often very quickly find themselves out of sync with the other cell members, whether they quit, are ostracized, or simply move among the leaders to deal with the disorder and its delusions of grandeur.

Those having the characteristics noted were preoccupied with fantasies of limitless brilliance, power, and success, and had an embellished sense of self-importance that was not commensurate with their actual level of achievement. They had no empathy and were not able to identify with the needs of others. They were envious of those with advantages that they did not have and believed that others were jealous of them. They needed a great deal of appreciation and constant approval from those who followed them.

Notation

This makes them so much harder to profile. The accused may become genderless, ageless, and without national limits during imprisonment for long periods of time.

Successful profiling is best sought when professionals seek the truth about the accused and from the accused through a holistic picture fashion.

If we are looking at the complete person, we must take everything into consideration, be it cognitive, emotional, behavioral, physical, or even the environmental factors that surround the person in question.

Although we humanly disapprove of the acts of violence and terror, as professionals we must set aside our opinions, biases, and prejudices to be able to perceive the truth. Stained lenses may only see the color of one's own lenses, not the actual paint of the other.

Even when there is an explanation,
there is never an excuse.

Chapter 4

Psychopathic Terrorists

There is a popular notion that an individual who engages in terrorist-related activities must be experiencing a kind of severe mental illness. A terrorist is assumed to be suffering from bouts of insanity, or to be a psychopath. This assumption is often made by the general public due to the general consensus that no typical human being could or would, in his right mind, inflict intentional harm and death on civilians on a large-scale level. It is often assumed that

1. The terrorist is not in their right state of mind at the time of the act of terror and is in need of mental health assistance.
2. The terrorist is an emotionless psychopath who does not have any remorse or guilt.

When seeking to understand the psychological profile of the psychopathic terrorist, it is important to make these distinctions clear. First, *insanity* is a legal term regarding a defendant's ability to determine right from wrong when a crime is committed. When discussing this concept in psychological terms, we understand that the individual is unable to distinguish reality from fantasy, is experiencing psychosis, or does not possess the cognitive processes to understand right from wrong at the time of the crime. According to the *Diagnostic and Statistical Manual of Mental Disorders, Fifth Edition* (DSM-5) (APA, 2013), the field of psychiatry classifies this inability as manifesting from severe mental illnesses such as schizophrenia or other psychotic disorders, major depression or severe forms of other mood disorders, or developmental disorders such as intellectual disability or autism spectrum disorders, whereby the individual does not possess sufficient cognitive capacities to ascertain right from wrong. (Note: It must be highlighted that individuals with intellectual disabilities and autism spectrum disorders have rarely been involved with cases of terrorism. If involved, they are more likely to be the scapegoat of a terrorist act, and are as prevalent within terrorist populations as within nonterrorist populations. In addition, individuals experiencing psychotic or severe mood disorders are no more likely to participate in terrorist-related activities than mentally healthy individuals.)

With regard to the second notion that terrorists are psychopaths, a further clarification must be made between the terms *psychotic* and *psychopathic*. *Psychotic* refers to individuals who have lost touch with reality, as can be experienced by individuals diagnosed with schizophrenia or other disorders involving a loss of reality. On the other hand, *psychopathic* refers to the DSM-5's antisocial personality disorder (ASPD) diagnosis, a classification previously termed "psychopathic personality" and "sociopathic personality." For this reason, the terms *psychopath* and *sociopath* have been frequently used in colloquial language when referring to individuals with ASPD. These distinctions have been made to clarify that a psychotic or "insane" individual is one who would likely be unable to differentiate right from wrong of the committed act. Alternatively, a psychopathic individual is one who is able to understand that distinction yet continues to engage in his remorseless actions for self-gratification, with no regard for other individuals. For the purposes of this chapter, the term *psychopathic terrorist* is used to examine the profile of the terrorist possessing certain traits of ASPD. (Note: The pronouns *he, him*, and *his* are used in this chapter when referring to the terrorist. While most cases of terrorism have involved males, there have been many accounts of women partaking in terrorist-related activities. The use of male pronouns will only be in reference to the terrorist and is not suggestive that terrorism is only a male activity.)

In the DSM-5, the diagnosis of ASPD highlights the following:

There is a pervasive pattern of disregard for, and violation of, the rights of other individuals, as well as authoritative figures. Key behavioral traits of Antisocial Personality Disorder include manipulation to achieve one's ends, frequent deceitfulness, lacking concern, guilt or remorse about the harmful effects of one's own behaviors on others, and persistent feelings of anger, or irritability to minor or perceived slights. Moreover, individuals with this personality profile tend to have a disregard for obligations or commitments in their lives and are more likely than not, to engage in risk-taking or thrill-seeking behaviors. In addition, a pattern of impulsivity may be manifested by the individual's failure to plan things ahead of time. Lastly, those with this personality profile tend to experience very little to no intimacy or empathy with other people and their behaviors are typically driven from an ego-centric, self-directed sense of self (APA, 2013).

Due to these personality traits, individuals with ASPD fail to conform to social norms or lawful behavior. They may repeatedly engage in impulsive, risky behaviors that are grounds for arrest (whether they are arrested or not), such as destroying property, harassing others, stealing, or pursuing illegal occupations. Moreover, they are likely to be unsympathetic to others and may provide superficial reasoning for hurting or mistreating other people. As a result, they are unlikely to make amends for their behaviors and are more likely to repeat their behaviors in the future.

This pattern of behaviors is likely to begin in early adolescence, where the individual has a tendency to engage in aggressive behaviors toward other people, such as bullying or getting into physical fights, deliberately destroying objects or property, or engaging in theft or deceit. Some of these disruptive behaviors can even be traced back to childhood where, as young children, these people express anger and become defiant toward figures of authority or with rules and social norms. When expressed in childhood or adolescence, these disruptive behaviors are classified as conduct disorder and oppositional defiant disorder. If they continue to persist into adulthood, these behaviors often escalate, leading to an ASPD diagnosis.

As with many psychological disorders, ASPD is understood as having a genetic and environmental etiology. Therefore, research suggests that when children are genetically vulnerable to possessing antisocial tendencies, they are also likely to experience child abuse, neglect, inconsistent parental discipline, and may come from unstable or chaotic homes. It is likely that their parents were acting on their own antisocial tendencies when raising them. As a result, there is the increased likelihood that their conduct problems in childhood evolve into antisocial traits when they reach adulthood.

A quick look at the DSM-5 criteria for ASPD easily lends to the notion that all people with the disorder must be criminals, typically engaging in illegal activity. However, this is not always the case, as many individuals with antisocial traits live their lives without criminal activity, raise families of their own, and have successful careers. Some career paths that attract people with antisocial traits include CEOs, attorneys, surgeons, and journalists. However, it is important to note that a large portion of individuals with ASPD do in fact choose criminal paths. So therein remains the question: Are terrorists psychopaths?

There has been much debate regarding this question, and the answer is a lot more complex than a simple yes or no. Not all terrorists are psychopaths. That is, many do not fit the criteria of someone with an ASPD. However, there are a number of terrorists that share some personality traits with someone with ASPD. It is this terrorist whose personality profile will be referred to as the psychopathic terrorist.

Similar to other people with ASPD, the psychopathic terrorist is amoral in that he lacks a moral compass, making him unconcerned with behaviors that would be considered right or wrong. The psychopathic terrorist is nonethical due to him lacking a fully developed superego (i.e., the psychopathic terrorist does not possess a conscience that reflects learned societal standards and morals within his environmental context). In addition, the psychopathic terrorist is able to deliberately make use of a person or situation to his own benefit. In doing so, he exploits the other unfairly in order to ensure that his own agenda is being served. Thus, manipulation and the exploitation of others are characteristic of this type of terrorist.

The psychopathic terrorist also shares some traits with narcissistic personalities, in that he feels an inflated sense of self-importance, feels an extreme desire for admiration from others, and lacks any understanding of how other individuals feel. As a result, he experiences an exaggerated sense of superiority toward other people, making it easy for him to engage in violent terror attacks on others. Individuals with high levels of narcissism continuously crave the admiration of others. Contrary to the popular belief that they possess high levels of self-esteem, these individuals are often emotionally damaged and have suffered psychological childhood injuries. When they do not receive the attention they crave, they often feel humiliated. In a terrorist, this trait can be highly dangerous as their response will be to react with aggression, or even with violence.

Unlike terrorists who possess socio-political-religious motives, the psychopathic terrorist utilizes a political or religious cause as an instrument, which serves as the means to reach his end goal (i.e., the political or religious motive is merely the tool, rather than the cause, for his antisocial tendencies, and is used to fulfill his destructive desires) (Crenshaw, 2000; Tanay, 1987; Victoroff, 2005). The psychopathic terrorist is biologically predisposed to engaging in violent activities. It is these terrorist activities that allow him some form of outlets for his antisocial tendencies so that he can engage in gratuitous violence (Brannan, Esler, & Strindberg, 2001). Well-renowned psychoanalyst Sigmund Freud theorized that aggressive behavior stems from the life force "Eros" and the death force "Thanatos." It is through a perceived threat that the psychopathic terrorist attempts to create a balance within himself by directing the death force outward to other individuals. It would seem that the psychopathic terrorist engages in terroristic violence in order to preserve his own sense of self (Corrado, 1981).

Typically, terrorists have specific targets as the victims of their terrorist cause. These targets are typically within the civilian population, or members of states or governments. At most, terrorists target anyone who isn't fighting for or on the side of their terrorist cause, creating an *us versus them* dynamic. However, unlike other terrorists that have specific targets as their victims, the psychopathic terrorist does not. Rather, he is nondiscriminative in targeting his victims because he does not maintain an internal belief system of any political or religious cause.

For the psychopathic terrorist, his source of gratification arises from his need to feel superior to others, regardless of who the victim is. There may be the possibility of specifically targeted victims, particularly if the psychopathic terrorist is a hired gun for a larger terrorist organization. However, if needed, the psychopathic terrorist will harm any individual who may be perceived by him as a threat to his sense of authority.

In addition to all these characteristics, it is important to note that the psychopathic terrorist is typically male, whose age tends to be within early to late adulthood. It is unclear as to why this is the typical demographic of the psychopathic terrorist. Moreover, similar to individuals with ASPD, the psychopathic tendencies tend to decrease when the terrorist is well into his fifties. It is possible that he still possesses antisocial characteristics, but may be less inclined to act on them due to the physical limitations that come with old age.

As earlier stated, the psychopathic terrorist possesses traits of narcissism where he experiences self-centeredness and entitlement, as well as a sense of superiority over other people. Moreover, in his exaggerated self-importance he lacks the ability to perceive another person's point of view or empathize with others. Therefore, in terms of types of terrorist activity, the psychopathic terrorist is highly unlikely to be involved in a plot that requires him to sacrifice his life. It is doubtful that he would engage in a suicide attack or mission as he holds himself in high regard to be sacrificed for any socio-political-religious cause.

Interestingly, the psychopathic terrorist type has been observed in some terrorist bombers. Psychodynamically speaking, psychopaths are characterized by a grandiose sense of self-worth, are driven by an aggressive narcissism, and lack any guilt or remorse for their actions. In exploring a few cases of terrorism, these traits can be observed in terrorist bombers. One such example of psychopathy is observed in Theodore Kaczynski, famously known as the "Unabomber." In statements made in his "Manifesto," Kaczynski justified his entitlement to kill people in order to have his ideas widely spread, to be acknowledged and admired. The fact that he believed the widespread death of civilians was justifiable for his own personal gain is clearly indicative of his grandiosity and callousness. Moreover, he presents as lacking remorse for his actions, as he was able to carry out his violent actions, after much pondering in his Manifesto.

There are some arguments suggesting that psychopathy is not consistent with the behavior of terrorist bombers. This argument stems from the idea that psychopaths tend to be impulsive, while the act of bombing is typically one that requires the terrorist to engage in a planned and calculated behavior in order to execute a successful attack. While it might appear so, it would seem that both terrorist bombers and those with psychopathic traits do not understand the long-term consequences of their actions. Another argument indicative of the psychopathic profile and bomber being inconsistent is the manner in which the attacks are executed. It would seem that bombers do not come into direct contact with their victims due to the very nature of the terrorist plot. This appears somewhat inconsistent with the psychopath, who, more sadistic in nature, is more likely to directly hit their victims. Another point of discrepancy is that a bomber uses technology, such as a bomb or explosive device, in order to make a political or religious statement stemming from his own belief system, while a psychopath's actions do not appear to be value driven. Once again, it is important to note that while the psychopathic terrorist does not necessarily have an ASPD, he will share some traits of psychopathy.

Therefore, he may possess some traits of psychopathy and not others, and may vary in the degree of these antisocial traits (Silke, 1998). The greater the number and degree of antisocial traits he possesses, the less likely are his terrorist-related crimes to be motivated by any internalized political or religious belief system. Another point to note is that the psychopathic terrorist may not present similarly as an individual with ASPD. It is likely that they may share the genetic traits of antisocialism, although his antisocial tendencies may present differently. It is likely that his sadistic needs are gratified through his role as a terrorist bomber (Meloy & McEllistrem, 1998).

Some argue that psychopathy and terrorism are two separate areas of study, and that terrorists do not meet the criteria for an ASPD diagnosis. The argument is that although terrorists often commit egregious acts, they themselves are not necessarily psychopathic and, more often than not, present with normality (Heskin, 1980; Shaw, 1986). However, to suggest that there is no collection of specific personality traits that influence one toward the career path of terrorism is to suggest that there is absolutely no subconscious or hidden psychological influence in the terrorist's decision to join the terrorist cause. While it is unlikely that the psychopathic terrorist is an individual with a clinical ASPD diagnosis, it is plausible that this terrorist profile possesses many psychopathic traits (Crenshaw, 1986). It would seem highly unlikely that within an organization, based on creating fear through means of mass murder and torture, are individuals who are not misanthropic in nature. Some forms of antisocial traits have their place within terrorist organizations, allowing for individuals with these dispositions to be drawn to terrorism (Meloy et al., 2001). One clear-cut example of psychopathic traits in a terrorist is illustrated in Nezar Hindawi, a Jordanian terrorist who, upon sending his pregnant girlfriend on a flight to Israel, had a bomb planted in her luggage, unknown to her. This terrorist clearly demonstrates psychopathy in that he was willing to sacrifice his girlfriend and his unborn child, with callousness, and no sense of remorse in doing so.

Other arguments against the psychopathic model as an explanation of terrorism state that the demands of a terrorist lifestyle do not fit with the personality characteristics of a psychopath (Kfir, 2002). Those with psychopathic tendencies tend to be impulsive and exhibit a sense of grandiosity and self-admiration. Terrorism, on the other hand, supposedly requires one to be dedicated and calculated in their efforts to carry out a terrorist attack, often selfless for their cause. While the two appear to be inconsistent, there is no indication that psychopathic traits are not present in terrorist profiles.

Other scholars argue that a psychopath and terrorist are two different beings. This argument stems from the idea that terrorists are involved in what could be construed as a group activity toward social annihilation, as opposed to resulting from internal desires for destruction. Yet, a multilayered perspective of the etiology of terrorism indicates that the psychopathic terrorist may use an ideological cause to express his own individual psychopathic cravings. Additionally, it should be highlighted that not all terrorist activities are group related and can be the direct result of one individual, particularly in cases of domestic terrorism.

As earlier stated, the psychopathic terrorist is one who possesses traits similar to those of individuals with ASPD, without necessarily meeting criteria for a clinical diagnosis. However, very high levels of psychopathy can negatively influence their chances of recruitment into a terrorist organization. Given that such individuals are unpredictable, impulsive, and guided by their own selfish needs, they are not very likely to participate as members of a group. Terrorist groups require members who will not be a liability for the group, do not cause high suspicion, and who can carry out the tasks assigned to them. Simply put, terrorism, as with any group dynamic, requires that each member play their specific role without disruption. Therefore, it would seem that terrorists would not likely hire many members with psychopathic tendencies. However, terrorist groups use violence as a means to achieve their goals. Thus, there are some recruited group members with psychopathic tendencies, playing the role as "hired guns" for the organization (Heskin, 1985). It is also possible that the psychopathic terrorist can be a top leader or the one leading the terrorist organization. If the leader of a terrorist organization is in fact a psychopathic terrorist, he is likely exploiting and manipulating his group members in order to achieve his own needs.

Defense Mechanisms of Psychopathic Personalities

Individuals possessing psychopathic personality traits are those that are impulsive and are unable to delay gratifying their instinctual needs. A person with psychopathic traits does not simply engage in attacking society, but believes that society obstructs him in getting his needs met. From a psychoanalytical perspective, this individual possesses a superego that appears to be flawed, if not absent. As a result, he often engages in behaviors that fulfill the needs of his id impulses—that is, the individual's basic, instinctual drives that motivate him to seek pleasure. However, since the psychopathic terrorist does not live in isolation, he is often challenged with regard to his socially unacceptable behavior (e.g., engaging in violent terror attacks). In order to alleviate or avoid unconscious conflict between socially accepted behavior and his own id impulses, he is likely to engage in what psychoanalysts refer to as defense mechanisms. A psychopathic terrorist would have a tendency to engage in the following defense mechanisms:

1. *Denial*—This defense mechanism occurs when the terrorist is in denial of his external reality. When in denial, it affects how he perceives his external reality; he sees what is happening, yet refuses to acknowledge his own perceptions

of the situation. Often, the psychopathic terrorist simply refutes what he has seen or heard. Moreover, he is likely to deny criminality and other involvement with other terroristic-related activities. He may make statements like "There is no way I did that. I have no idea what you are talking about."

2. *Distortion*—Distortion helps the psychopathic terrorist to grossly reshape his external reality in order to meet his inner needs. These inner needs are likely to be unrealistic megalomaniacal beliefs, wishful delusions, and sustained feelings of his delusional entitlement or superiority over others. In order to maintain these inner needs, the psychopathic terrorist will likely distort facts of the external world in order to maintain his distorted views and beliefs. In light of a terrorist attack, he may say, "They were fine. Nobody was hurt," when, in reality, there could have been many targets who were injured as a result of his violence.

3. *Projection*—This occurs when one attributes their own thoughts and impulses onto another person. This usually occurs when the individual cannot accept the thoughts, feelings, or impulses he or she experiences, thereby projecting them onto other individuals. This defense mechanism is not uncommonly used by individuals experiencing delusions. The psychopathic terrorist will make "you statements," thereby accusing his opponent of being involved with criminal and/or terrorist-related activities. He is likely to see himself as the victim rather than the perpetrator. He is likely to make statements such as "I am not the terrorist. You are the one causing terror. You are the reason for all this destruction." In such an instance, he is essentially blaming his opponents for his own destructive behavior. If involved with a religious or political terror group, he may use their ideologies to blame oppositional religious or political groups for the destruction from their own violent attacks.

4. *Projective identification*—This type of defense mechanism is similar to projection in that the terrorist deals with emotional conflict or internal stressors by projecting his own intolerable thoughts, feelings, or impulses onto other people. However, it differs from projection in that the psychopathic terrorist remains aware of his own thoughts, affects, or impulses. This in turn creates a conflict for the person because he cannot admit or accept the emotions, thoughts, or impulses, yet he cannot help but be aware that these exist in him. Therefore, in order to satisfy his own needs, he explains his unacceptable behavior as a justified reaction to his opponent's behavior. "Yeah, I did that, but only because of what you all did to me."

5. *Acting out*—This is a direct expression of the unconscious wishes or id impulses that are forbidden by the superego. The unconscious fantasy is literally acted out through impulsive behavior, thus gratifying their inner needs. When the individual engages in this type of defense mechanism on a more chronic level, it allows him to avoid the internal stressors he would experience from postponing his urges to act on his impulses. The psychopathic terrorist, who possesses a flawed superego, is likely to act impulsively on his needs

as he does not have internal prohibitions to prevent him from acting out. In such an event, the act is likely to be deliberate, in that he does not care about the consequences of his acting out. When he is confronted with the wrongful act, he will try to protect himself by engaging in other types of defense mechanisms, such as denial, to protect himself from shame, or distort his perceptions of his external reality to suit his inner needs.

6. *Rationalization*—This defense mechanism is one that incites the individual to use logic to justify his unacceptable behaviors, thoughts, or feelings to reassure himself of his actions and avoid experiencing feelings of anxiety, guilt, or other negative emotions. The psychopathic terrorist is likely to engage in rationalization to justify his violent actions in order to avoid dealing with feelings of shame and guilt resulting from the wrongdoing of his violent crimes. The psychopathic terrorist is likely to be unconsciously aware of his wrongdoing, and in justifying his actions, he can even convince himself to believe that what he is saying is true. He may make statements such as "I did it because it was the right thing to do."

7. *Devaluation*—The individual using this defense mechanism to cope with unconscious conflict is likely dealing with emotional internal or external stressors. Typically, an individual with psychopathic traits tends to engage in devaluation of others by exaggerating the other's negative qualities in order to make the other people feel as if they are flawed or worthless. In individuals with narcissistic tendencies, devaluation is followed by a long period of idealization (when the person expresses exaggerated positive attributes of the other individual). For a terrorist within an organization, this defense mechanism may be used by him in order to recruit, and later gain control over, lower-ranking terrorist members.

8. *Passive aggression* (turning against the self)—When engaging in this type of defense mechanism, the individual deals with internal or external stressors or emotional conflicts by unassertively, indirectly, and/or occasionally self-detrimentally expressing aggression toward others.

Case Example

PP-1, a 27-year-old male from Lebanon, was imprisoned on two counts: first, for accusations of establishing an armed organization, and second, for being involved in abductions where he transported people from Estonia to Syria.

PP-1 was the youngest among five sisters and three brothers. His father was in the Lebanese Army and was "always absent." His mother had grown up in a village in Lebanon and was reported to be a traditional woman. PP-1 was raised by his elder sister, whom he was very fond of, and stated was more important than his mother and father. In grade 4, PP-1 had thrown himself from the second floor of his school building when his teacher had aggressively hit him on his hands with a wooden ruler. PP-1 had left school during grade 7 to work with his father and cousins in the clothing industry. At the age of 17, PP-1 went with his friend to Iraq, where he witnessed his friend being shot in his mouth and killed by the U.S. Armed Forces. He reported that he always remembers his dead friend.

PP-1 later began working as a truck driver and married at age 21. After 8 days of marriage he was detained for establishing an armed organization for which he was imprisoned in the Roumeh Prison, where he said he had met a lot of people from the Al Qaeda group. In his late 20s, PP-1 became a smuggler between Syria and Lebanon by using his truck. He transported people from Estonia to Levant. His wife, a Shi'a, became a Salafist after his imprisonment, wearing the full dress of a Salafist, "covering herself from head to foot with black." PP-1 believes that this is the proper Islamic attire for women. They have a daughter and a son.

During the interview, PP-1 frequently yawned and appeared to lose his train of thought. He appeared to be depressed when talking about his family and had reported feeling sad, especially when his wife and children visited him in prison. He mentioned that his wife subtly blames him for his absence from the family. PP-1 had a variable vocal intonation from high to midrange. He spoke within a normal pace but would suddenly elevate his voice tone when an intelligence officer passed by the interview area. PP-1 experienced physical trauma when he was shot 12 times by the Lebanese Army—in total, he had 2 bullet shots on the side of his head, 1 bullet shot near his heart and lungs, 2 bullet shots in his right arm, 2 bullet shots in his right leg, and 5 bullet shots in his back right thigh. He appeared to have an exaggerated startled response from bullet sounds and shivered from just recalling the sounds of bullets. When the topic of the intelligence officer would arise, PP-1's right leg would shake.

During the interview, PP-1 appeared to engage in defense mechanisms typical of the psychopathic terrorist. During a previous interrogation, PP-1 was in *denial* of facts regarding his 12 bullet wounds. Furthermore, PP-1 engaged in lying when he was asked about the other people who were accused with him in the Estonian abductions. PP-1 gave three different scenarios during the interview:

1. He did not know them before the interrogation.
2. He knew them when they asked for transport smuggling to Syria but said that he did not know that there were people involved in illegal trade.
3. Later on, PP-1 said that two of "those people" were his friends and died during the interrogation with the Lebanese intelligence officers.

PP-1 appeared to be pseudoaltruistic in that he appeared to pretend to care for others when he spoke. However, he also engaged in *projection* by expressing his aggression toward others indirectly through passivity, masochistic behavior, and turning against his own self. PP-1 appeared to minimize his role in terrorism but amplify the "fault" of the others involved. He indicated that he could not have done better or differently because others in his life were to blame. PP-1 appeared to almost want people to feel sorry for him. Yet, his psychological profile highlights that he was not ideological or rigid and inflexible. His specific goals were selfishly set, with no loyalty to a particular group. He appeared to only care for his own welfare, at the expense of others, indicating a certain degree of narcissism. It is possible that the physical damages to his brain may have influenced his mental state or may be partially responsible for the behavior in question.

Given that PP-1 fits the profile of a psychopathic terrorist, the following recommendations were made: (1) PP-1 is provided the opportunity of rehabilitation to direct and guide him to a nonterrorism mentality and find an option of a legal lifestyle. (2) PP-1 should not be released from prison until he has achieved a successful rehabilitation. This success would be determined by a qualified committee of experts in criminal psychology or forensic psychology. (3) In addition, if PP-1 is released from prison, he must be monitored for a legal probationary period of time. It has been suggested to authorities that reliable sources for information regarding PP-1's childhood could potentially be used in remediation.

Identifying a Psychopathic Terrorist

While defense mechanisms are internal mental processes, they can be behaviorally observed through the types of statements one makes. In the case of the psychopathic terrorist, he can be identified by his statements of denial, projection, distortion, devaluation of others or by him acting out. In addition to defense mechanisms, one can identify the psychopathic terrorist, usually if he presents with a history of consistent rule breaking, a tendency for risky behaviors, lacking empathy, callousness, and a lack of remorse or guilt for any behaviors that were harmful to others. As earlier mentioned, a person who presents himself as superior to others can be someone potentially fitting the profile.

In addition to observing these traits, as well as direct statements indicating the above-mentioned defense mechanisms at play, one can identify a potential psychopathic terrorist through his body language. Individuals, who cross their arms, particularly with their fists clenched, tend to exhibit signs of hostility and defensiveness. This combined posture is suggestive that the individual is in an aggressive mode and prepared to attack. Another gesture indicative of suspicious activity is when the individual displays their thumbs up while folding their arms. This posture is usually observed in individuals who want to portray themselves as being in control of a situation, while at the same time trying to maintain some protection over themselves. This posture is typically the sign of self-confidence or of an individual portraying a superior attitude. Other postures typically associated with aggression are closed palms, while defensive postures include a lack of hand gestures, keeping one's hands close to oneself, or maintaining an overall closed body language. An individual with the psychopathic terrorist profile will act out his life by exuding body language of high superiority. In this way, he can reveal himself, and be likely identified as a possible terror suspect.

In addition to body language, the items carried or clothes worn could be indications of a possible terror suspect. Some items indicative of suspicious activity may involve wearing clothing that is inappropriate for the weather (e.g., wearing a long jacket or heavy clothing during the summer), wearing clothing with a lot of pockets or jackets that appear to have items stuffed inside, handling packages delicately, leaving packages unattended in public spaces, or moving toward the center of large crowds with packages or backpacks. Moreover, individuals carrying a weapon or a firearm in a public area could be an indicator of aggression, especially if the person is observed to be holding it close to them. When attempting to identify a person with this profile, it is important to note that one single presentation of these traits, defense mechanisms, or body language cues is not indicative that the individual is a psychopathic terrorist. Rather, it is the accumulation of multiple indicators that would suggest the person identified is likely to fit the profile. The greater the number of indicators, the more likely the target will fit the profile of a psychopathic terrorist.

Risk Assessment of the Psychopathic Terrorist

While the field of forensic psychology has been able to develop risk assessment tools for violence in accurately predicting domestic violence, sexual assault, and physical violence, terrorism has proven to be a different type of criminal act, serving a different psychological function among those who engage in it. While there have been some risk factors to identify potential terrorism, there has not been sufficient research examining these risk factors with terrorism. However, with regard to the psychopathic terrorist, one can utilize specific psychological assessment tools and skills in determining the levels of risk for an individual with this profile. In doing so, the following risk factors need to be kept in mind when conducting a risk assessment with this profile:

1. *Age*—The mean age of violent terrorists ranges from around 20 to 29 years. There appears to be some variation over the mean age across different parts of the world, where Middle Eastern terrorists typically tend to be in their early 20s, while terrorists in other populations, such as the Chechens, tend to be in their late 20s. This age range appears to be a factor for the psychopathic terrorist, as psychopathic traits tend to be prominent in the early years of adulthood.
2. *Gender*—Most psychopathic terrorists tend to be male, as is also commonly found in individuals with ASPD.
3. *Marital status*—There is a tendency for the psychopathic terrorist to be unmarried. While the terrorist lifestyle tends to conflict with that of maintaining a marital status, it is also important to remember that the psychopathic terrorist tends to lack intimacy or empathy with other people, and is therefore likely to be unmarried due to being unable to form social connections with other people.

4. *Social class*—While there is not much empirical evidence to suggest a correlation with terrorism and social class, individuals possessing traits of ASPD have a higher likelihood of coming from a lower socioeconomic status and lower family income and may also have a lower education level (this might be particularly true if the psychopathic terrorist exhibited truancy during childhood).

5. *Prior crime*—While this may not be typical of other terrorist profiles, the psychopathic terrorist is likely to have a history of involvement in violence, which may not necessarily be related to terrorist activities. It is the lack of empathy for others, engagement in risky behaviors, and lack of conformity to social norms that make it likely that a person with this profile will have a criminal history. It is possible that he may have been raised in a family where aggression and violence were normalized for him, resulting in him easily engaging in violence himself.

Although there are no specific assessment tools in identifying the psychopathic terrorist, certain measures could be incorporated to help aid the process. The Historical, Clinical, Risk Management–20 (HCR-20), a risk assessment for violence, was developed to help professionals make structured decisions regarding the probability of violence in people with criminal histories. This measure consists of three areas:

1. *Historical area*—This area examines the background of the potential terrorist by taking into consideration factors such as previous violence, age at first violent incident, alcohol or substance use problems, psychopathy, and early family or social disruptions in childhood.

2. *Clinical area*—This area examines the potential terrorist's level of insight, attitudes, presence of symptoms of mental illness, impulsivity, and level of responsiveness he might have to treatment.

3. *Risk area*—This area examines the stress level, presence or lack of a support system, and exposure to substances and alcohol.

The Hare Psychopathy Checklist–Revised (PCL-R) is another assessment tool that is used to measure a person's antisocial or psychopathic tendencies. The PCL-R can be used alongside the HCR-20 in determining whether the potential target at hand fits the profile of a psychopathic terrorist by assessing one's psychopathic tendencies as well as risk of violence.

However, while these assessment tools are able to determine the level of risk these individuals pose in terms of violence, there are challenges in determining their level of risk of involvement in terrorist-related crimes, as there are no specific tools to identify crimes related to terrorism. Additionally, there is no evidence that current psychological assessment measures or tools have been used to identify the likelihood that a specific target fits the profile of a psychopathic terrorist. In addition to commonly used psychological measures, an inquiry into the person's exposure to firearms or explosives, access to funds, and current political ties can provide the assessor a clearer picture about the person's level of engagement in terrorism. When assessing the level of risk, the assessor must utilize the results derived from assessment tools. However, the assessor must go beyond those results and incorporate collateral sources and social information regarding his political and religious ties, as well as use one's clinical judgment regarding the potential target they are assessing. Together, all these sources of information could be indicative of whether the individual being assessed is involved with terrorism and could determine their level of risk in engaging in violence (Borum, 2015).

Negotiations with a Psychopathic Terrorist

The psychopathic terrorist is an individual who is narcissistic and unconcerned with the welfare of others. In addition, they are only interested in their own personal benefits. While they can be hired by a terrorist organization to be the "hired gun," they acquire little to no interest in the ideological cause they are working for. Therefore, they can kill anyone who they perceive as a threat, and will do so with no remorse. Negotiating with the psychopathic terrorist can be extremely difficult because they have no concern for their hostages or for any other individuals involved. However, as challenging as this task may be for law enforcement, it is still possible to walk through a successful negotiation with a terrorist of this profile type. When negotiating with the psychopathic terrorist, it is important to keep in mind that his first priority is himself.

Therefore, the negotiator should be able to convey to the psychopathic terrorist that, should any hostage be killed or harmed, there will be negative consequences that will directly impact the terrorist's own personal interests. Therefore, even if he is working for a larger terrorist organization with an ideological cause, he is likely to abandon the larger terrorist plans if his own gains are at risk. In doing so, the negotiator will have the upper hand in being able to carry out negotiations.

It is essential for the negotiator to build rapport with the terrorist, particularly if the situation involves targets being held as hostages. While the psychopathic terrorist holds no concern for his hostages, it is possible that he may display a charming persona toward them. Assessing for Stockholm syndrome is vital, especially if the crisis is drawn out for a long period of time, as it could increase the chances of hostages experiencing feelings of affection and trust for the terrorist. If hostages develop positive feelings toward the psychopathic terrorist, this can be dangerous and can interfere with the successful capture of the terrorist, as hostages with Stockholm syndrome may work with or even risk their own lives to help the terrorist. It is also important to keep in mind that since the psychopathic terrorist holds himself as his first priority, any threats of suicide over capture are more likely to be false than true.

Previous cases of hostage negotiation have indicated that offering payment in exchange for hostage safety and return has not been successful, particularly for the psychopathic terrorist. This is because his motivation is derived more from an instinctual need for sadism and less from one that is monetary in nature. Typically, when terrorists make demands, a state or government does not provide any concession to appease them. This is usually the case with most governments taking a stand on not negotiating with terrorists. Additionally, complying with the terrorist can be challenging due to the impracticality of the demands that are often made. However, this should not stop the negotiator from letting the terrorist think that his demands are being met. Even if it is not practically possible to comply with the terrorist's demands, making him believe that the negotiation is on the way allows the tactical team to buy some time in order to diffuse the crisis.

In order to carry out the negotiations, law enforcement teams need to begin by breaking down the big demands made by the terrorist into smaller ones. This can be achieved by cutting off the terrorist's most basic needs, such as cutting off access to food, water, electricity, and possibly all means of the terrorist's contact with the outside world (i.e., blocking off all access to wireless Internet connections and other data signals to prevent communication from him to the larger terrorist organization). This would also prevent him from gaining access to the media regarding the crisis situation. Rather than acting immediately, negotiators should utilize stalling and delaying techniques to allow the terrorist time to require these needs. Over time, terrorists will feel tired and require basic needs, including food, water, and basic physical comfort. Tangible items, such as food, water, and electricity, can then be used in making negotiations with terrorists. In doing so, negotiators will be successful in breaking down big demands into smaller ones they can comply with. However, when utilizing stalling techniques, it is important to keep in mind that the psychopathic terrorist is one who is impulsive, and his potential for inflicting harm should not be ignored.

While operating in such a crisis situation, there need to be successful communication strategies between the negotiator and the terrorist, as well as between the negotiator and the tactical teams. In maintaining successful communication, the negotiator must be able to have direct and clear forms of contact with the terrorist. If there is a language barrier between the terrorist and negotiator, it is imperative to find a highly skilled interpreter to translate the negotiations. However, in a more ideal situation, the negotiator would be the individual who is able to speak the language of the terrorist. This can avoid any disruption in the flow of communication and can further help the negotiator build rapport with the terrorist. Moreover, a team of negotiators, or at least a pair, is likely to lead to a more successful negotiation, as opposed to just one negotiator. Any crises situations involving terrorists are highly stressful, and negotiations can be drawn out for long periods of time; therefore, a team can allow for each individual to take breaks when needed, and can reduce the stress and burden of the task at hand.

Additionally, there needs to be an organized form of communication between the negotiators and the tactical teams, with neither team being in competition with the other. When a terrorist-related situation occurs, all crisis management teams need to be able to cooperate with one another so as to allow all team members access to the appropriate information. Ideally, during training, hostage negotiators should work with, and be familiar with, members of the tactical teams, as well as translators, to allow for easier collaboration.

The use of deadly force in a terrorist-related situation should be considered a last resort. If during negotiations a hostage is killed, it is likely that further negotiations will be fruitless. Negotiators should be able to make an accurate judgment when negotiations are no longer beneficial and allow tactical members to take over the situation. It is important to remember that while there are strategies that law enforcement officials can utilize during a terrorist hostage takeover, they serve as guidelines and might not be successful in every situation.

Identify the Psychopathic Terrorist Characteristics

Age varies
Amoral (lacks superego)
Criminal type
Excitable
Exploitive
Impulsive
Insincere
Intelligent
Irresponsible
Manipulative
Narcissistic
No general goals in life
Nondiscriminative targeting
Nonethical (lacks superego)
Personality disorder
Untruthful
Nonsuicidal

Chapter 5

Ethnogeographic Terrorists: Religious and Political

Fundamentalism is defined as a strict maintenance of traditional orthodox religious beliefs, a religious movement that developed among various bodies based on strict adherence to certain tenets (Allen, 1986). This definition can be applied to political as well as religious fundamentalism. To understand the fundamental mind-set, let us look at ourselves in terms of attribution theories. According to Fiske and Taylor (1991), "attribution theory deals with how the social perceiver uses information to arrive at causal explanations for events." It looks at the information gathered and how it is merged to create a fundamental judgment. It deals with how and why common people give explanations to events as they do.

Religious and political terrorists exhibit the same or very similar dynamics, but for different causes. In explaining others' actions, professionals frequently commit the fundamental attribution error. We attribute their behaviors so much to their inner dispositions that we discount important situational forces. The error occurs partly because our attention focuses on the persons, not on the situation. A person's race or gender is vivid and attention getting; the situational forces working on that person are usually less visible.

When we attempt to explain individual or group behavior, such an attribution error renders biased conclusions that may severely distort our results (Pettigrew, 1979). We tend to attribute positive characteristics and legitimate justifications to actions taken by our own group members, and attribute negative characteristics to actions done by others. For illustration, if an individual within *our* social group fails to pay a certain donation, we will believe that they have certain legitimate circumstances preventing them from doing so, while if they are an *outsider*, they will be viewed as stingy, selfish, or lacking a good heart. "This inclination to over exaggerate the influence of behavior, personality traits, motives, etc. and underestimate the power of external factors in a given situation is known as the fundamental attribution error or FAE" (Amabile, Ross, & Steinmetz, 1977; Saylor.org, n.d.). Often, this is a product of the cognitive strategy used to abridge and easily process the information of the intricate world. An observer may have very little familiarity with the context of the situation and possible environmental or social limitations. In effect, the person will depend more on character factors in order to clarify and comprehend the particular situation. Psychologists took notice that when language is used to depict the behavior, rather than the situation, it often becomes richer.

Fundamentalist terrorists view the world within the narrow lens of their own ideology, be it Marxism–Leninism, anarchism, nationalism, Islamic fundamentalism, or some other ideology.

In his book *Psychology of Terrorism* (2004), Randy Borum succinctly details considerations regarding ideologies and the notion of a collective belief system that outlines, explains, and validates a shared set of rules and values:

> For terrorists, ideology helps to provide "the moral and political vision that inspires their violence, shapes the way in which they see the world, and defines how they judge the actions of people and institutions" (Drake, 1998). To state simply that ideology controls actions (which may generally be true), does not explain why or how that control occurs. This is a relevant consideration because it is the strength of behavioral control—not just the appeal of the rhetoric—that determines whether violent mandates will be followed. Taylor (1991) has provided perhaps the clearest behavioral explanation: "the way ideology controls behavior is by providing a set of contingencies that link immediate behavior (e.g., violence) to distant outcomes (e.g., new state, afterlife reward)." Because the connection is distant, however, to exert any effect, the contingency must be absolutely certain (hence the need for unquestioning acceptance). In addition, the outcomes or rewards need to be powerful motivators or reinforcers. That is, they need to be fervently desired.
>
> In contrast, compliance with religious rules appears to be maintained only by "escape contingency,"—the prospect of reducing or eliminating the feelings of guilt or fear the religion has caused the noncompliance to evoke. (Mallot, 1988, 196)

The thought is that ideologies, and religious ideologies in particular, may include moral and divine mandates that often compel—if not require—adherents to action.

Borum goes on to state:

> Skitka and Mullen (2002, 46–47) define moral mandates as "the specific attitude positions or stands that people develop out of a moral conviction that something is right or wrong, moral or immoral. Moral mandates share the same characteristics of other strong attitudes—that is, extremity, importance and certainty—but have an added motivational and action component, because they are imbued with moral conviction." The divine mandate is one of the unique—and potentially most concerning—features of the extremist driven by religious ideology. As characterized by Rapoport (1983), "the transcendent source of holy terror is its most critical distinguishing characteristic; the deity is perceived as being directly involved in the determination of ends and means." In her extensive study of 250 Palestinian terrorists and recruiters, Nasra Hassan noted that all of them believed that their actions were "sanctioned by the divinely revealed religion of Islam." Finally, in an analysis of the connection between ideology and violent action, Taylor (1991) posited a combination of three key factors as having particular importance:

> > *Militant potential*—(i.e., whether violence is legitimized in the ideology as a means to an end);
> > *Totality of the ideology*—(i.e., extent to which the ideology controls all behavior, not just specific religious or political elements); and
> > *Perceived imminence in millenarian achievement*

Cognition is an essential concept in psychology since it is the process of acquiring knowledge and understanding about the world through experience. Cognitive theory emphasized that an individual's intellectual activities, such as perception, memory, and reasoning, are significant determinants of behavior. In most of the research, fundamental "terrorists generally do not regard themselves as terrorists but rather as soldiers, liberators, martyrs, and legitimate fighters for noble social causes. Those terrorists who recognize that their actions are terroristic are so committed to their cause that they do not really care how they are viewed in the outside world. Others may be just as committed but loathe to be identified as terrorists as opposed to freedom fighters or national liberators" (The Psychology of the Terrorist, n.d.). "By having moral imperatives as their goals, the fundamentalist terrorists perceive the world through the distorted lens of their religious beliefs. Although the perceptions of the secular Arab terrorist groups are not so clouded by religious beliefs, these groups have their own ideological imperatives that distort their ability to see the world with a reasonable amount of objectivity. As a result, their perception of the world is as distorted as that of the fundamentalists. Consequently, the secular groups are just as likely as the fundamentalist groups to misjudge political, economic, and social realities" (The Psychology of the Terrorist, n.d.; see also Hudson, 2018).

Referring to Kohlberg's Scale (a theory that moral reasoning and ethical behavior consist of six developmental stages), fundamentalist terrorists would fall in the lower spectrum and be categorized with a lower level of emotional and cognitive development (Larsen, 2007). These persons tend to fall within the first few levels: preconventional, conventional, and postconventional, which are characterized by

- Obedience and punishment orientation
- Interpersonal conformity
- Authority orientation and social order maintenance
- Universal ethical principles

Within this primitive stage of cognition, individuals tend to surrender to an authority and lack critical or individualistic thinking. Their low cognition is what leads them to believe that they should follow an authority, usually blindly. This also facilitates the psychological manipulation of such individuals by political and/or religious authorities. Kohlberg argues that only at higher stages does an individual engage and think in a responsible or democratic way, rendering them capable of engaging in a positive negotiation.

To put the nature of violence into the proper context, recognizing the dynamics between religion, politics, and society is vital. The change from patriotic violence to fundamentalism should be identified by an individual, and then how fundamentalism has become the core of current terroristic activities explained. Taking part in one's definition are his cultural identity, sociopolitical realities, and religious association (Rausch, 2015). These factors create complexities in expression within generally understood terms. As a result, there are several motivations causing terrorist attacks on innocent victims. These motivators may include, but are not limited to, political, social, moral, personal, and religious. "Terrorism has been used all through history and throughout the world by states, organizations, groups and individuals" (Ali, 1997). Although there are various motivations in the rise of present-day terrorist attacks, religious motivation is found to be a main source of terrorism. D'Souza (2009) writes, "So there is little wonder the claim that religion is awful and leads to violence." "It is certainly true that many horrible things have been done under the cover of religion—the inquisition springs to mind along with Islamic terrorism and the Catholic–Protestant wars that have raged and influenced European and American politics for centuries" (Desai, 2013; see also Valencia et al., 2011).

In his article "Religion and Terrorism: A Socio-Historical Reconsideration," Okoro Kingsley (2010, 554) references the "clash of civilization" as a key factor in the current rise of global violence, but that history has shown religion to be the greatest cause of terrorism historically:

> The escalation of global violence—terrorism associated with religion and her institutions—is an ever-present reality with us. Islamic religion

all over the world has been alleged as the gravest architect of religious violence vis-à-vis terrorism. Therefore, Senghal (2003) opines that Muslims continue to push their communities into medieval practices and as such they pose challenges to communal harmony and perpetrate the backwardness of their community. Therefore, the clash of civilization is being provoked by Islamists in many parts of the world. In this direction, Avolos (2005) asserts that religious terrorism is indeed caused by religions, or rather that religion creates an imagery supply of sacred resources over which human beings contend. Accordingly, Avolos (2005) regards all forms of social and political conflicts to be a contest over scarce resources. The ones who do not have the scarce resources want them and the ones that have them want to keep them. In relating this postulation to religious conflict, Avolos (2005) maintains that the scarce resources are the things that religion specifically supplies, which include the favor of God, blessing and salvation. These are the graces not bestowed equally on everyone and must be earned and protected (Okoro, 2008).

Dulles (2002) further observes that Christianity has had more than a fair share of religious tensions in human history. Christians have persecuted Jews and fought wars against Muslims, within Christianity; there have been internecine wars, especially between Roman Catholic and Protestants, but sometimes with Eastern orthodox. Influenced by these postulations, casual observers accept as fact, even in western culture, that religion is the worst culprit of the global terrorist attacks (Okoro, 2008).

These characteristics may be illustrated in the followers of many religious groups having the sense of a messianic or apocalyptic dream in their political vision, which comprises the thought of political dominance of a state (or the world) through its association. Believers of these groups take the dream of future prominence gravely, where power and control compensate for their present deprivations. There are cases where messianic fantasies are shifted into political action plans. When the ideology of fundamentalism is altered from a religious belief into a political ideology represented in a political movement, it becomes of importance for politics—even more so when this political movement gains political power of mass support.

With regard to the fatality of fundamental terrorism, the prevalence of suicide tactics must be considered. Fundamentalist terrorists believe that they are more likely to succeed, knowing that they will die because of the act of terror. The idea of self-sacrifice is greatly rewarding, which empowers the fundamentalist terrorist to take more risks and be more destructive. To rationalize their actions, they create new methodologies. Most often, this includes death or self-sacrifice, which leads to their search for martyrdom. Terror has become their way of life, where peace becomes a threat to their very existence. These characteristics lead to increased violence as the fundamental terrorist committing the terroristic act has become fearless of ramification from authorities.

Borum stresses that research suggests no major psychopathology among suicide bombers or would-be attackers. Those clinical phenomena found in suicide cases differ dramatically from the factors and motives of individuals who perpetrate suicide attacks. In our modern world of asymmetric wars and conflict, suicide attacks—or campaigns of attack—could be deemed as having "strategic logic" (Borum, 2004).

Silke (2001) contends that "as with other terrorists, there is no indication that suicide bombers suffer from psychological disorders or are mentally unbalanced in other ways. In contrast, their personalities are usually quite stable and unremarkable (at least within their own cultural context)."

In some ways, the absence of suicidal risk factors among suicide attackers is not surprising. They are different phenomena (Borum, 2003). Suicide attackers view their act as one of martyrdom, whether for their faith, their people, or their cause. In the case of jihadists, for example, Salib notes that "the primary aim of suicide terrorists is not suicide, because to the terrorist group, suicide is simply a means to an end, with motivation that stems from rage and a sense of self-righteousness. They see themselves as having a higher purpose and are convinced of an eternal reward through their action" (Salib, 2003, 476). The act of sacrificing to further the cause of Islam (in their view) is seen as the highest reward to the actor. The act is seen as martyrdom, and the actor a martyr by immediate family and community: those "true believers" loyal to the cause. That ultimately is the underlying motivating factor.

In a study conducted by Townsend (2007), it was concluded that various terrorists do not show any particular evidence, as a group, of psychological disorder, nor do they have personality traits in common other than "enmeshment with religion." Rather, indoctrination and group processes are the commonly cited motivations. A key point that was stressed throughout is that a terrorist's suicidal behavior is instrumental rather than an end in itself. The individual is not much trying to end his or her own life, or to avoid negative feelings, but is trying to accomplish a political goal and concurrently enter paradise. Group processes reinforce this belief and keep the individual committed to his or her path. The belief that one is entering paradise appears to be sincerely held by Muslim terrorists. If so, then judging their affect, by how they appear at the time of the mission, seems to us to be an invalid way of assessing possible underlying psychological motivation (Townsend, 2007). Indeed, in Meloy's (2004) psychological autopsy of Mohammad Atta, one of the leading 9/11 terrorists, he finds rather extensive symptomatology in Atta's background. Atta's conflicted relationship with his father and his excessive dependency on his mother would provide any Freudian with ample evidence of an unresolved Oedipal complex. Meloy (2004) himself concludes that Atta's immersion in extremist religious doctrine and his decision to martyr himself were driven by repressed sexuality and displacement of intense anger toward his perfectionist father. The idea that deep religious involvement functions as an outlet of strong emotional conflict echoes Schbley's (2003) concept, referred to as "dogma-induced critical/psychotic depression."

Defense Mechanisms of Fundamentalist Types

Fundamentalist terrorists perceive the world differently from how society and members of the government do. Their reactions and approaches to government policies are guided by their ideologies. Their actions are founded by their subjective interpretation of the world, rather than an objective reality, and their conviction may seem irrational or delusional to society in general, but they may nevertheless act rationally in their commitment to act on their convictions. Therefore, a fundamentalist terrorist may have the tendency to use the following defense mechanisms:

1. *Introjection.* In *Ego Mechanisms of Defense,* Vaillant clearly articulates this concept: "With a loved object, the terrorist uses this defense mechanism through internalization of characteristics of the object, with the goal of establishing closeness to, and constant presence of, the object. Anxiety consequent to separation or tension arising out of ambivalence toward the object is thus diminished. Introjection of a feared object serves to avoid anxiety by internalizing the aggressive characteristics of the object, thereby putting the aggression under one's control. The aggression is no longer felt as coming from outside but is taken within and used defensively, turning the person's weak, passive position into an active, strong one. Introjection can also rise out of a sense of guilt, in which the self-punishing introject is attributable to the hostile destructive component of an ambivalent tie to an object. The self-punitive qualities of the object are taken over and established within one's self as a symptom or character trait, which effectively represents destruction" (Vaillant, 1992). In fundamental terrorist groups, their intensified group introjections lead very sternly in incorporating new political or religious ideas or doctrines, as if the sole identity of their group feeds on those to keep its presence.
2. *Passive-aggressive behavior.* "This involves the terrorist's aggression toward an object, expressed indirectly and ineffectively through passivity, masochism, and turning against the self. This defense mechanism is a less obvious form of abuse" (Vaillant, 1992). This issue arises when the individual can't seem to find a way to manage their anger in a normal or healthy manner.
3. *Projection (immature).* This occurs when the terrorist takes his or her unacceptable qualities or feelings and assigns them to other people. With the core emotion of hate being found at the root of this unconscious behavior, it includes severe prejudice, rejection of intimacy through suspiciousness, hypervigilance to external danger, and injustice collecting. "Projection operates correlatively

to introjections; the material of the projection is derived from the internalized configuration of the introjects" (Vaillant, 1992). Shared projection magnifies the present dangers posed by others.

4. *Schizoid fantasy.* "This is the terrorist's tendency to use fantasy and to indulge in autistic retreat for the purpose of conflict resolution and gratification" (Vaillant, 1992).

5. *Reaction formation.* A mechanism in which the terrorist substitutes behavior, thoughts, or feelings that are diametrically opposed to his or her unacceptable ones. It is converting unwanted or dangerous thoughts, feelings, or impulses into their opposites.

6. *Intellectualization.* The individual deals with emotional conflicts, or internal or external stressors, by the excessive use of abstract thinking or generalizing to avoid experiencing disturbing feelings. John Grohol, in his piece "15 Common Defense Mechanisms," states, "Intellectualization is the overemphasis on thinking when confronted with an unacceptable impulse, situation, or behavior without employing any emotions, whatsoever, to help mediate and place the thoughts into an emotional, human context. Rather than deal with the painful associated emotions, a person might employ intellectualization to distance themselves from the impulse, event, or behavior" (Grohol, 2016).

Case Example 1: An Ethnogeographic Religious Terrorist

EG-R is a 39-year-old male from Palestine. During the interview, he wore an Afghani outfit and appeared to be clean with his long beard. He was frowning most of the time and was speaking in normally with a high-pitched tone. EG-R has been in prison for 7 years, accused of the United Nations Interim Force in Lebanon (UNIFIL) explosion in 2009.

EG-R was raised in a poor environment at Ayen el Helwi camp. As he recalled, he had bad memories of his father. At the age of 10, his father would beat him in front of their relatives. His father would also burn EG-R's hand with cigarettes whenever he would do something wrong. Since then, he's been resentful toward him. At a young age, EG-R's father abandoned the family and married another woman. From then on, EG-R and his brother were solely raised by their mother, who opened a small bakery to support their financial needs. He dropped out of school when he was 17 years old and started working to help his mom. He was a handyman and most of his occupations were carpentry-related.

At the age of 24, EG-R's brother recruited him to join the Ahl al Dawa movement. He didn't stay for long since he sought change and later joined Al Qaeda. Subsequently, he's been in trouble with the Lebanese government and was a runaway for 14 years. During this time, he met his wife, got married, and had four children. EG-R had an unstable relationship with his wife and children. In 2009,

EG-R was imprisoned. He became aggressive and would easily get mad at things; thus, he made a lot of trouble. Because of this, he avoided communication with the other inmates.

From the brief history of EG-R's profile, his patterns of relationship were quite noticeable. He was engaging in *projection* as a defense mechanism. Considering his childhood trauma and experiences with his father, the core emotion of hate has brought him to this unconscious behavior. This was manifested in his relationship with his wife and children, where he assigned his unacceptable qualities or feelings, such as rejection of intimacy through suspiciousness. This brought about insecurity in their family relationship.

Furthermore, his *passive-aggressive behavior* was also evident, where he would deal with his internal or external stressors or emotional conflicts by unassertively, indirectly, and/or occasionally self-detrimentally express aggression toward his inmates. This caused him to isolate himself in his cell whenever he would be sad or mad.

When asked about his plan after his release from prison, EG-R mentioned his desire to "finish his mission." Thus, *schizoid fantasy* is evident. He uses this fantasy and indulges in autistic retreat for the purpose of conflict resolution and gratification.

Case Example 2: An Ethnogeographic Political Terrorist

EG-P is a 45-year-old male from Palestine. During the interview, he was neatly wearing a veil and his ankle-length abaya. His hair was shoulder length and he had a medium-length beard. He kept a high-pitched tone and normal speaking voice. EG-P was accused of three bombings in Tripoli (north of Lebanon). EG-P also admitted that another accused terrorist took refuge at his home for 3 months at the time Al Abbsi was injured.

EG-P was raised in Bedawi camp, a Palestinian camp in Tripoli. His father was an Imam who frequently stayed in the mosque and would only spend 3 days with them at home. EG-P fondly recalled that he used to play sick during his father's visit so he could get all his attention. His mother was uneducated, but he remembered her to be a smart lady. However, she was fragile and sickly because she had a heart problem and diabetes. At a young age, he always had the fear of losing his mom. His mother died when he was 22. EG-P had four sisters and seven brothers. At the age of 6, one of his brothers died. He recalled how terrifying it was for him to witness the Islamic death ceremony.

EG-P gave his first speech as an Imam when he was 17 years old. He always had his father's encouragement. Later on, at the age of 22, he became an official Imam at a mosque in Bedawi camp. He studied religion and took Islamic Sharia in his first year. He had difficulty finding a job as a nurse at Lebanese hospitals because he was a Palestinian. He was finally hired as a nurse at an Islamic hospital where he worked for 15 years. As an Imam, EG-P was known for his fiery speeches. He would constantly clash with Palestinian political parties, such as Fatah and Hamas. EG-P is married with three children (two sons and one daughter). Since he was close with his father, EG-P and his wife had him move in with them when they got married. EG-P felt sad while he talked about his family. He felt like he abandoned them since he was imprisoned. To make certain that his family feels his presence, he always takes the opportunity to communicate with them via phone calls. He also mentioned that at present, he gives much attention to his sons.

In prison, EG-P was assigned to be one of five committee members. He was in charge of the medical and social section. Although there were cases of prisoners being beaten up or whipped as punishment, EG-P was not given such punishment when he confessed about sheltering another accused terrorist since he did not lie before the judge and the interrogators.

During the interview, it was also noted that EG-P appears to be funny and sociable. He likes to go around and visit other floors in the prison. He was also very fixated on his religious belief. Throughout the conversation, he would mostly refer and connect everything to his religion. EG-P also expressed his need to take control of things. He gets mad and furious when he is not in control. These characteristics reflect EG-P's use of *reaction formation* as his defense mechanism. He seems to be converting his unwanted or dangerous thoughts, feelings, or impulses into their opposites. It could be exasperating for him to be imprisoned, losing the power to be in control of things around him, and he would have the need to get out of jail. Instead, he is cooperative with authorities and sociable and funny around his inmates. He may be incapable of expressing his negative emotions of anger and unhappiness with his situation, and instead becomes overly kind to publicly demonstrate his lack of anger and unhappiness.

Profile of a Religious Terrorist

The following is an abridged, select set of characteristics, derived directly from Schbley (2003, 105–134), intended to create a profile for identifying a religious terrorist:

1. Most religious terrorists choose to commit self-immolation around religiously significant anniversaries.
2. As a religious terrorist becomes committed to the act of self-immolation, he or she exhibits signs of serene disengagement. These signs of snapping or detachment from their secular milieu are marked by a faint smile, distant look, lack of eye contact with the interviewers, disciplined or submissive body posture, and what appears to be a contentment or inner peace with imminent face.
3. Religious terrorists committed to self-immolation would attempt to follow strict dogmatic rules of conduct to maintain their perceived purity and

qualification for heavenly admissions. They would speak in the plural, refrain from vulgarity, perform all religious and secular obligations, and pay all legal debts.

4. Before their self-immolation, a religious terrorist would not indulge in earthly pleasures (e.g., gambling, sex, liquor, and dance).

5. A religious terrorist's target would most likely be well defined and limited in scope and dimension and would not transcend a concentric target zone.

6. Non-self-defensive acts of violence distinguish religious terrorism from those acts committed to fighting for religious freedom.

7. The potential religious terrorist has an affinity for martyrdom, is not averse to risk, and is a risk-taker.

8. To a religious terrorist, perceived religious obligations or divine messages transcend social consciousness and social obligations.

9. Most religious terrorists' beliefs are based on their interpretations of charismatic religious leadership.

10. Most religious terrorists who have committed or are willing to commit suicide missions are between the ages of 13 and 27, are from poor families, and are geoculturally immobile.

Schbley further differentiates the religious from the political terrorist by asserting that—due to both the aforementioned characteristics and their indoctrination—a religious terrorist may not be aware, understand, or ascribe maliciousness to their own actions. The rational being of their death and their victims' deaths are temporal. Religious terrorists are serving both as executor and prophets for their deity and believe that their sacrifice will ensure their place in the heavens.

Risk Assessment of Fundamentalist Types

The following risk factors must be considered when conducting a risk assessment with this profile:

1. *Age.* In recent times, there have been an increasing number of adolescents joining fundamental terrorism. The adolescence stage can be psychologically difficult. During this period, a person begins to have self-awareness of being a separate, fragile, and vulnerable individual. This results in an adolescent's strong need of belongingness and identity, which is why they often become avid followers of a fashion trend or pop groups and join gangs. Belonging to certain groups eases their sense of separateness and builds up their identity. However, this also makes them vulnerable to religious extremism. Religious affiliation and belonging to a terrorist group within that religion offers a concurring community, sharing common beliefs and probably gives them a

family-like structure. It may also serve as a statute-seeking opportunity for those who are deprived or may have little or nothing in the common society.

2. *Social class.* There is not much empirical evidence to suggest a correlation with terrorism and social class. However, for this type, they may be from either poor families or a refugee camp. Those who aren't from these backgrounds are by-products of the migration of middle and lower-middle class college-bound high achievers into economically stagnant urban slums (Ansari, 1984).

3. *Childhood and adult experiences.* Just as there is no single terrorist personality or profile, a specific constellation of life experiences is neither necessary nor sufficient to cause terrorism. The role of life experiences in understanding a pathway to terrorism is based mainly on certain emotional and behavioral themes. In the contemporary literature three experiential themes appear to be robust: Injustice, Abuse, and Humiliation. They often are so closely connected that it is difficult to separate the effects and contributions of each. By definition, most abuse is unjust. Humiliation often results from extreme forms of abuse (often involving the anticipated judgments of others). Moreover, those experiences may have different effects when they present in different forms (e.g., parental abuse vs. prison abuse) or at different points in one's development (e.g., during childhood vs. during adulthood) (Borum, 2004).

4. *Motivation and vulnerabilities.* There is no easy answer or single motivation to explain why people become terrorists. Similarly, the processes and pathways of *how* that happens are quite varied and diverse. Researchers have begun to distinguish between reasons for joining, remaining in, and leaving terrorist organizations, finding that motivations may be different at each stage, and not even necessarily related to each other. There do appear to be some common vulnerabilities and perceptions among those who turn to terrorism:

    a. *perceived injustice*
    b. *need for identity*
    c. *need for belonging* (Borum, 2004).

Negotiations with Fundamentalist Types

To better negotiate with the ethnogeographic types, know your own biases first. Learn to block them out to maintain a clear and more objective role in negotiating. Issues of transference and countertransference are manifested here. The ethnogeographic players work as part of a group. The group in itself enhances the goals to destroy "the common enemy." Their motto is "to die for the cause is an honor." Those who die with them, voluntarily or not, will also be rewarded in the afterlife, youthful martyrdom, or both. So, negotiation to kill or harm them is their means to an end and therefore of no benefit to the negotiator.

Clinical experience with such persons and individual members of groups has suggested passive-aggressive characteristics. The symptoms of passive-aggressive personality disorder all revolve around the central theme that the person with such a disorder is sabotaging efforts directed at getting him or her to work or socialize at an expected level. Usually, such people think they are doing better work than they really are and get very angry when others make useful suggestions about how their performance might be improved. They tend to be critical of those in authority.

This person, or individual within the group, asks for help but then does not comply with the advice or evidence of cooperation.

Guy Olivier Fauer and I. William Zartman (2011) in their book *Negotiating with Terrorists: Strategy, Tactics, and Politics* outline key points for negotiators in dealing with fundamentalist types:

1. Recognize that they are beyond any negotiation and attempts to deal with them directly are pointless. The point is to identify potential conditionals, encourage them to see the hopelessness of their situation and the potential hopefulness in responding to negotiations.
2. Address the issues beyond the terrorism. Terrorism is ultimately related to such structural issues as poverty and inequality that are far beyond any immediate remedy. But steady attention to related issues of importance to potential supporters may eventually reap rewards.
3. Do not negotiate a belief system. In the course of implementing the outcome of a negotiation it may be possible to instill doubt about the basis of motivating beliefs, but the negotiation itself needs to focus on specific items.
4. Recognize that unlike many hostage/kidnapping situations, the acts of fundamentalist terrorists are not self-contained events. Hence negotiation is not an autonomous subject or policy, but a long process.
5. Respect is the basic condition of any negotiation. 'One-down' approaches that seek to impart a sense of inferiority are unproductive.
6. Effective negotiations can begin when the parties perceive themselves to be in a mutually hurting stalemate and see a way out. Maintain pressure (stalemate) while offering a way out. Show terrorists that there is something to gain from negotiation.
7. Mediation is often necessary: the mediator can both carry messages and formulate ideas. Neither party trusts the other, but both must trust the mediator for mediation to work.
8. Identification, separation, and moderation are the general aims of negotiation with terrorists. Identify those who seem open to talks. Split moderates from extremists by emphasizing alternative means to the moderates at a lower cost than the use of terror. Moderation is a process and not a condition of negotiation. Engagement in negotiation, and the new situation it produces, can gradually produce deeper changes, but this will take time.

They go on to state:

> Investigation, contact, and communication are the general means of negotiation with absolute terrorists. Find out as much as possible about the terrorists' values and goals. Establish and maintain contact. Contacts are the crux of negotiation. Building contacts will doubtlessly be in secret, but must be backed by public statements indicating openness to negotiate. Use step-by-step agreements to advance terrorist negotiations. Negotiation is a matter of giving something to get something; hence, the negotiator needs to offer the terrorist concessions to his demands as the payment for his abandonment of violent terrorism. The terrorist, too, must make concessions, and the absolute terrorist does have something to offer as payment—his choice of terrorist tactics. (Faure & Zartman, 2009, 3–4, 2011)

Identify the Ethnogeographic Terrorist Characteristics

Close family ties
Displaces word *wrongdoing* with the word *war*
Educable
Egocentric
Emotional priority for the cause
External superego
Familial conditioning and loyalty
Ideological
Inflexible
Intelligent
Male or female
Suicidal—martyr "for the cause"
Rigid
Seeks control
Specific goals set
Youth or young adult

Chapter 6

Retributional Terrorists

The understanding that there may be a category of terrorists independent of psychopathic, political, and religious motives came to the author during his work with victims and perpetrators of war. The term *retributional terrorist* was devised by the author based on his realization that certain individuals become terrorists to seek vengeance for past personal trauma (Hamden, 2002). During the last 5 years, the author consulted and provided direct clinical treatment to victims of war, directed a major public affairs committee on the Middle East, and provided testimony to the U.S. Congress (House and Senate) on these issues. Part of the task was to interview persons who participated in the crises of their respective nations.

These interviews, along with research, confirmed the initial idea of retributional terrorism and revealed that (1) political and religious fighters had ethnogeographic concerns, (2) the psychopathic terrorists were outcasted by the other fighters because of the seemingly nondirected type of goal behavior, and (3) the retributional terrorists had completely different motives from the others. The identification of the retributional terrorist was initiated while individually interviewing 30 subjects—27 males and 3 females—with a structured, nonstandardized interview and mental status evaluation technique. Some of the interviewees had been reportedly involved in direct terroristic acts, such as bombings, while most of the others interviewed had only fought in militias (political or religious—Christian and Muslim) alongside terrorists and suicide fighters. There was reportedly no emotional or social pathology in their psychological development, and no familial conditioning to political or religious ideology. However, these individuals, purely and discriminately, sought retribution for a particular trauma they suffered in the past.

Retributional Terrorists: A Psychological Explanation

Retributional terrorists seek revenge for past trauma inflicted on themselves or loved ones. These individuals have been victims of war and suffered great losses at the hands of war. These losses translate into a depleted sense of self and a threat to one's ego, and accordingly activate the ego's survival instinct, compelling the individual to strive to retain their sense of self and self-esteem (Knoll, 2010). In simpler terms, sufferings of war pose as a threat to one's survival, both physiological and psychological, which motivates the ego toward survival. However, an injured ego often harbors resentment toward the abuser and over time results in the need for revenge. This revenge is a survival tactic that protects the individual from future sufferings at the hands of the perpetrator. It is also a mechanism by which the individual can retain their identity and sense of self.

There also exists a psychophysiological reason as to why the retributional terrorist might seek out revenge against the offender. Seeking revenge, or even the idea of seeking it, activates the dorsal striatum—the area of the brain responsible for processing rewards (de Quervain, et al., 2004). Hence, the mere thought of avenging past trauma induces positive feelings in the mind of the retributional terrorist. Moreover, upon seeking revenge, the urge to further avenge only becomes stronger. According to Bushman (2002), venting anger results in increased levels of aggression. This suggests that the retributional terrorist is trapped in a cycle—seeking revenge, acting in vengeance, and acquiring an increased thirst for revenge following each act of vengeance. This is evident in the actions of most retributional terrorists who join terrorist organizations for personal motives but endure in the organization because their desire for revenge is not satisfied.

To better understand the psychological aspect of retribution and terrorism, focus must also be placed on the childhood of a retributional terrorist. Early childhood is a crucial time period in the life of such individuals. Children born in families of terrorists, as well as victims of war, have a difficult childhood. They may be faced with abandonment, humiliation, negligence, and the lack of a parental figure (Kobrin, 2016). These individuals are likely to have suffered the absence of a father while growing up. The father may have died, abandoned them, or been negligent toward the children, causing a severe negative impact on the child. In the absence of a father, the mother of these individuals is responsible for their upbringing, followed by older siblings and relatives. This is evident in the case of the two men who committed the Boston Marathon attack: Dzhokhar and Tamerlan Tsarnaev. During the childhood of the Tsarnaev brothers, they were faced with the absence of their father. Due to this, Tamerlan, being the eldest son, resorted to taking care of his younger brother, Dzhokhar. As the brothers grew up taking care of each other, they developed a strong bond. Similarly, the retributional terrorist may have a close family member with whom they share strong bonds. However, there may not be a strong bond with the biological father.

There may also be a significant early-life trauma in the life of a retributional terrorist. Traumatic incidents such as physical, sexual, verbal, emotional, and psychological abuse have a severe impact on the worldview of a retributional terrorist. These incidents may lead them to view the world as a hostile and threatening place, prompting them to be cautious and seek revenge from those who harm them.

As the world appears to be a threatening place for retributional terrorists, these individuals are protective of themselves and close family or friends. This caution is both conscious and subconscious. On a subconscious level, the individual's caution is manifested in the form of defense mechanisms. According to Sigmund Freud, defense mechanisms protect an individual's innermost emotions, vulnerabilities, and insecurities from the harshness of reality. Some defense mechanisms are used consciously, meaning that they are deliberate and intentional. However, most defense mechanisms operate unconsciously or subconsciously, and lie outside of our awareness (Trevithick, 2011). Understanding how defense mechanisms are used helps us understand how retributional terrorists deal with conflicts and negative events in daily life. Moreover, these unconscious mechanisms give insight to the vulnerabilities of the terrorist, enabling authorities to negotiate and have a rational conversation with them.

Retributional terrorists have four major defense mechanisms that they use to protect their ego from reality:

- Controlling
- Rationalization
- Anticipation
- Intellectualization

Controlling

Controlling is a basic mechanism that seeks to attain and maintain power over the situation in order to avoid or repress the feeling of being out of control. It is the excessive need to manage and control events, people, situations, or objects that allows the individual to feel better, minimize anxiety, and resolve subconscious conflicts (Vaillant, 1993). In the life of a retributional terrorist, this defense mechanism may manifest as a need to have every aspect of their life under control, including religion, personal, social, and terrorism-related activities. It may also be that this individual felt helpless during their traumatic past and controlling every domain of their current life will help them avoid feeling helpless and vulnerable again.

There also seems to be a link between this defense mechanism and the retributional terrorist's need for revenge. It's possible that the terrorist feels that they control the fate of the opposition by attacking or killing them. Thus, this mechanism may enable them to attain retribution.

Rationalization

This defense mechanism is categorized as a neurotic defense mechanism, indicating that when used repeatedly it negatively affects a person's mental state, conscious, and unconscious thinking patterns (Cramer, 2015). Rationalization involves justifying a thought or behavior that arises from repressed or deep-seated impulses, which are usually aggressive or sexual in nature (Trevithick, 2011). This justification is not necessarily for other people, but is instead for the person himself. By rationalizing one's unacceptable actions, an individual saves himself from negative emotions and anxiety that may arise if their deep-seated impulses were to surface. A retributional terrorist uses rationalization to justify his socially unacceptable actions. This individual may experience feelings of guilt and shame when attacking civilians. To decrease these negative feelings, he or she may suggest that the actions are for gaining leverage against the enemy, which provides justification for their actions.

Anticipation

Anticipation is a defense mechanism that involves creating a plan to avoid or repress a negative emotion. The individual anticipates that a negative event might occur and starts planning for possible physical and emotional actions they can take to avoid negative consequences. For example, a retributional terrorist may anticipate that they might be killed in the attack. Thus, while they are not opposed to sacrificing themselves for the attack, they may go to great lengths to form a plan that makes it more difficult for them to be attacked. Similarly, they may anticipate feeling deeply sad and guilty when performing terrorist activities. To avoid these emotional consequences, they would plan on building a cold exterior of anger, vengeance, and emotional apathy.

Intellectualization

Intellectualization is a neurotic defense mechanism that involves focusing on the intellectual or logical aspects of a situation and ignoring the emotional aspects. By concentrating only on facts and logic, an individual can distance themselves from the negative emotions that might arise from the situation. Intellectualization is used by retributional terrorists to avoid feeling empathy for the victims of their attacks. While attacking people, they may focus on statistics, race, religion, and ethnicity of the people to avoid focusing on the victim's emotions, pain, and suffering.

Retributional Terrorists: Psychological Profiling

This account is based on the several cases involving victims of war and the author's interviews with individuals who fought in third-world crises or were engaged in acts of international violence and crime.

Subjects were male and female of varying ages. They were educated, well-established, and functioning members of society. These individuals had moral and social principles that they adhered to, even during negotiations. While many of them met the criteria for mental disorders, they were never formally diagnosed. This may be because they have intellectualized and rationalized their past trauma, and hence do not consider it problematic. They also suffered from anxiety, but did not address it.

The onset of retribution was believed to be the result of a major traumatic incident that they were deeply impacted by. These individuals witnessed the slaying of family members while hiding during a massacre, or they had arrived to recover the bodies of loved ones and friends after a massacre. They were also witness to abuse and atrocities committed against their loved ones, which ignited feelings of anger and sadness. This in turn led to the desire to seek revenge, while also leading to feelings of hopelessness, helplessness, a lack of foundation due to family loss, and no destiny, goals, or future aspirations. These individuals were also stripped away of their social identity, and were deprived of social support provided by family or friends. With little or nothing to live for, they were voluntarily suicidal for their cause.

Developmental History and Adjustment

Physical and medical history revealed no pathology—meaning that they were typically developing. The usual childhood illnesses were experienced with no complications. Developmental milestones (walking, talking, bladder control, etc.) were met within a normal age range.

Childhood emotional and behavioral patterns were not reported or were uneventful. The individuals may have admitted to substance use (alcohol, drugs, cigarettes, etc.) at a social level but were reportedly nonabusive.

These young people were born into close-knit families. They were raised by both parents and had several siblings, some as young as 3 and 5 years old. The grandparents, aunts, and uncles lived in the same town. Friends and relatives gathered many times during the week for socials. The extended family included relatives and members of the community at large.

Educated through secondary schools and possibly a few years of university, some individuals could speak three languages fluently and performed well in science and literature courses. Having large numbers of friends and acquaintances, they showed positive social adjustment. All subjects liked school and displayed no disciplinary problems.

Resulting from a war or a crisis, severe economic losses were experienced and financial assistance came from a cultural welfare system. This caused personal humiliation for the individuals and remaining family members.

Some were married and had financial and emotional responsibilities to a spouse and children. Others were unmarried and had no children, thus having no responsibilities to any significant others.

Mental Status Evaluations

The individuals were alert but guarded. There were no peculiar mannerisms, tics, or tremors. They looked clean and neat. Their height and weight varied.

Speech patterns were relevant, coherent, and appropriate to the conversation when speaking both Arabic and English. Verbal productions were not impoverished but appreciatively dramatic. Their range of intelligence seemed to vary.

There were no signs of psychosis or neurological deficit. The prevailing mood tonality was blunted. Emotional swings were indicated due to the significant family trauma experienced. Signs of depression were clinically indicated. They were oriented to person, place, and time. Memory was intact. Insight was good. Judgment was not impaired.

Sleep patterns were reportedly marked by sporadic insomnia. Nightmares were suggested and related to the massacre of their family and friends. Feelings of guilt were associated with the individuals' feelings of impotence in not being able to stop the unjust crime against their significant others.

Trends of paranoia were reported in relation to general anxiety about the enemy, concerns of further attacks, and political paranoia about the nation/state.

Profile Summary

- Both genders (male and female)
- No age restriction
- No evidence of unusual developmental history
- Observed moral codes
- Very close family ties
- Sociable and disciplined
- Significant personal trauma in early life
- Adolescent patterns interrupted by war and necessary undertaking of militia role for economic/cultural survival
- Young adulthood process discontinued, leading to hopelessness, with little or no aspirations for marriage or family
- May first pursue retribution individually and later, post feelings of helplessness, join and adopt an ethnogeographic group (political or religious) for support
- Exhibit evident frustration from conflicts between conditioned motivation and unconditioned economic political restraints
- Lack self-control in vengeance, with an ability to discriminate between innocent victims and the sought target(s)
- Bright and intelligent, formally educated
- Evidence of appropriate adaptation and use of ego defense mechanisms
- Originate from various socioeconomic status situations
- Have at some point expressed feelings of alienation and discrimination

- Exhibit total loss of sensation and lack aspirations, with no future goals
- Aware that terrorism is a crime but hold strong beliefs that it is the only resort and method of avenging their loved ones and future aspirations

It is important to note that these characteristic features are not an exercise in diagnostic abnormal psychology. One may see such traits as symptoms. Therefore, this profile can assist in understanding the fourth type, but not in seeking out all terrorists.

Case Example 1: A Retributional Terrorist

EG-R1, a 32-year-old Lebanese male, was imprisoned at the age of 25 for allegedly providing aid to a prisoner, as well as helping a terrorist locate a bomb.

He is the oldest of four children and has three sisters and a brother. His father was a friendly man with a weak personality, while his mother had a strong, controlling, and dominant personality. He had a normal childhood and was favored by his mother due to him resembling his maternal grandfather.

In high school, he lost interest in education after being hit for the first time. Following his graduation, he joined the army school aiming to be a policeman, where he excelled and was honored more than thrice for being loyal. He later married and had a daughter.

His first encounter with fundamentalism took place in 2008, when Hezbollah tried to overthrow Beirut by sending fighters to kill non-Shiites. Being a Sunni himself, EG-R1 resented and begrudged Hezbollah, along with other Sunnis and Druze. The Sheikh leader of the Salafi group at the local mosque was acquainted with EG-R1 since childhood. He compelled another ally to help him by saying that if he did not, his family would burn in hell. EG-R1 was forced to help this Sheikh and was later imprisoned for this.

In prison, EG-R1 expressed anger at his unjustified imprisonment and admitted wanting revenge at the loss of his freedom. In the past, he had been depressed and suffered from an eating disorder after losing colleagues while disengaging a mine. To cope with this, he would laugh, smile, and try to cheer himself up.

His primary goal in life was to provide for and protect his family. He was also reportedly angry at the police for his faulty arrests. During the interview, he was generally polite and calm. He had a neat and clean appearance and reportedly hated being chubby or overweight.

Defense Mechanism Analysis

Humor: EG-R1 uses humor to cope with negative events in his life, such as the death of his colleagues. He admitted to smiling and laughing since there was nothing he could do to undo the wrong he did. Hence, his use of humor would provide him consolation and protect him from feelings of guilt.

Overcompensation: EG-R1 seems to have a fear of abandonment, neglect, and rejection. He may have also felt helpless and powerless in his situation. These fears may stem from the sudden turn of events during his adulthood, wherein he was no longer favored or protected by his parents. To compensate for these fears, he compulsively exercises and focuses on physical fitness. This physical fitness could have provided him with the assurance that he was strong and not powerless or helpless.

Anticipation and controlling: EG-R1 seems to expect bad things to happen to him in the future. This compels him to control every aspect of his life, include physical appearance, emotions, behaviors, and thoughts.

Summary

EG-R1 was a 32-year-old male prisoner, incarcerated for aiding a prisoner as well as a terrorist. He considered his incarceration unjust and expressed anger at this. He also expressed feeling helpless when forced to help the terrorist. Due to these circumstances, he was imprisoned and was stripped away from his freedom, family, and old life. He used a number of defense mechanisms, including overcompensation, humor, anticipation, and control.

While EG-R1 did not join a terrorist group for revenge, he seems to have retributional tendencies since he felt unjustly incarcerated and even expressed the desire to seek revenge. Hence, the following recommendations were made:

- EG-R1 should be given back his position in the police force and be assigned with teaching officers the terrorist mind-set. This will relieve him of the anger he had built up for his faulty arrests.
- EG-R1 should be granted amnesty for his wrongdoings.
- EG-R1's activities should be monitored to satisfy government questions regarding his intentions.

Case Example 2: A Retributional Terrorist

EG-R2 is a 20-year-old Syrian male who is incarcerated for his involvement in the Daraya explosion. He comes from a large family and has four sisters and five brothers. He has a strong relationship with his elder brother, who was also involved in the Daraya explosion.

As a child, EG-R2 was hit and beaten by his father in front of his relatives. This left him feeling deeply hurt and humiliated—a feeling he still recalls during his adulthood. His father was highly aggressive, and his mother was a very strict women.

Throughout his childhood, he liked drawing cartoons and admitted to drawing even now. EG-R2 recalls his school life being a calm period, wherein he refused to interact with women as it was considered unethical. At the age of 15, his interest in religion grew since he saw his elder brother becoming eloquent and receiving attention.

He later followed his brother and joined the Ahl al Dawa—a religious movement. He was later trained by an Al Qaeda trainer but was soon after arrested.

During his time in prison, EG-R2 disliked and refrained from interacting with the other prisoners, considering them impure people. He instead requested to have himself and his brother transferred to the terrorists' floor, but his request was denied. This sparked in him anger and resentment toward the authorities as well his fellow prisoners. When angry, he reportedly isolated himself to feel better. He reports his aim in life is to become an Imam and gain respect.

During the interview, his tone was low and he hesitated a lot. He also avoided eye contact as it was unethical.

Case Analysis

EG-R2 seemed to have a difficult childhood with his parents, especially his father. The physical abuse by his father left him with emotional scars that may have sparked anger in him. He also felt humiliated, and hence strived to be like his elder brother, who captured the attention of others and was eloquent.

As EG-R2 reached adulthood, the anger from his childhood was directed into religion and joining the religious movement. However, his arrest made him unable to work for the religious group, which aggravated his anger. He also considers others who are not a part of the Ahl al Dawa to be impure and has a strong affinity toward his own group of people. His anger and resentment grow when his requests in prison are denied. This may lead to him revolting against the authorities and seeking retribution. His desire to be an Imam may also be to satisfy his subconscious desire for retribution, as he could train a new generation of terrorists.

Defense Mechanism Analysis

EG-R2 seems to have used a number of defense mechanisms, including

- *Sublimation*: Sublimation occurs during his teenage years, when his anger, resentment, and feelings of humiliation are transferred into energy required in religious activities, to be like his brother.
- *Displacement*: EG-R2 harbors deep-seated anger toward his father, which is later on displaced toward the authorities. This may be because his arrest by the authorities brought back the same feelings of humiliation and helplessness he felt when he was abused by his father.
- *Rationalization*: EG-R2 refused to interact with other prisoners, citing the reason for his behavior as them being "drug addicts and impure." However, this may just be a superficial justification for his behavior. It appears that

EG-R2 has a strong tendency to surround himself with people of his own group as it may help him feel empowered, protected, and even respected. Hence, he refrains from interacting with the other prisoners as it is out of his comfort zone.

Identify the Retributional Terrorist Characteristics

Age varies
Close family ties
Educable
Ethical
Good use of psychological defense mechanisms, yet possibly explosive
Helplessness
Hopelessness
Intelligent
Male or female
May later join a support "group"
Moral history
No familial conditioning or loyalty to a particular group
No premorbid traits leading to personality disorder
Object relative
Significant early-life trauma onset
Discriminates targets
Social history with no legal problems
Suicidal "for personal reasons"

Chapter 7

Techniques of Interviews and Interrogations

Conducting *interviews* and *interrogations* and employing *interventions* are popular techniques used to get to know the accused.

Interviews

Interviewing is the less formal and less structured process of gathering details and information on a crime. Interviews do not have to be conducted in a law enforcement facility. Interviews follow a question–answer format. As interviews are one of the first information-gathering processes that take place, the interviewer generally assumes a nonaccusatory tone. It is the interviewee, not the interviewer, who speaks for a majority of the time during an interview.

Through interviews, the interviewer tries to ascertain who could be a potential suspect to a crime. These potential suspects may go on to be interrogated (Mueller, 1961). Victims and witnesses are also interviewed. Conducting multiple interviews with various interviewees highlights similarities and differences between each person's version of the events. Consequently, a more accurate and well-rounded picture of the crime from different perspectives can be attained.

Interviewers aim to make the interviewee comfortable so they are able to recount, with as much detail as possible, any and all crime-related information. Interviewees should be able to trust and have good faith in the interviewer, the lack of which could increase their resistance and unwillingness to communicate.

Interviewers may engage in a lot of note-taking during interviews as the interviewee recounts their version of events. Most interviews are short with a time limit set in place.

In the United States, the *Miranda warnings*, also known as the *Miranda rights*, must be given to a person when they are taken under police custody. Enforced by the Fifth and Sixth Amendments, they refer to one's right to remain silent and right to counsel, the latter of which can be sought or granted depending on one's financial circumstances. Interviewers are not legally obligated to declare Miranda rights during interviews.

The interview process is long and cumbersome as administrative arrangements need to be made for multiple individuals who have to be interviewed. Furthermore, investigators have to analyze each individual, along with the interview notes. However, the *broad* nature of analysis inherent in interviews is essential for the deeper and more *narrow, focused* progression of the investigation into potential suspects.

Interrogations

Interrogation is the more formal and more structured process of questioning a suspect, on a crime, so as to obtain a confession. Interrogations have to be conducted in a law enforcement facility. A majority of the time, interrogations assume an accusatory tone as by now the interrogator may have gathered evidence that points to the suspect(s) as being potentially guilty. Alternatively, interrogations can assume a nonaccusatory tone if the interrogator is still trying to gather more information from a potential suspect. It is the interrogator, not the suspect, who speaks for a majority of the time during an interrogation. There is no time limit set for interrogations. However, the lengthier the interrogation, the more likely the suspect can get fatigued, consequently impairing the quality and outcome of the interrogation.

Initially during the interrogation process, the interrogator ascertains whether the potential suspect is willing to be, and is being, truthful or deceptive. Based on this, the interrogation process proceeds to assume a questioning tone such that facts are verified and an admission of guilt may occur. Legally, it is not mandatory for suspects to answer any questions during interrogations, except for questions relating to their name and place of residence.

Interrogators do not generally engage in any note-taking during interrogations until the suspect makes an admission of guilt, after which the interrogator prepares a written confession. Sometimes interrogators may grow impatient or may be so consumed in the process of trying to elicit a confession/admission of guilt that they may employ unethical practices and exhibit unprofessional conduct during the interrogation process. Interrogation malpractices such as the use of torture and any form of degrading behavior and treatment are strictly prohibited across more than 100 countries, including the United States and United Kingdom (Human Rights Watch, 2003).

The word *interrogation* or *interrogate*, in itself, is a strong word that can elicit negative connotations of questioning a suspect in a forceful way. The news, media, movies, and TV shows portray interrogations in a way in which power dynamics are highlighted. The interrogator assumes a position of power, forcefully questioning or even manipulating the suspect to confess, in a way that some may consider quite dehumanizing.

To prevent ethical boundaries from being obscured, it is important to ensure that both interrogations and interviews are conducted in a humanistic, patient, and professional manner, such that the suspect is fairly and equally treated, the suspect is aware of their rights, and the suspect's rights remain withheld.

Interrogators are required to declare the Miranda warnings during interrogations. There is a divide in perceptions about whether the Miranda rights impair or enhance the process of criminal justice. This is because some believe that during interrogations, the guilty can use their Miranda rights to avoid a confession, impairing their conviction (Lassiter & Pinegar, 2013).

The criminal justice system cannot use instances where the suspect evokes their Miranda rights to incriminate. If a suspect asks for their lawyer to be present during an interrogation, the interrogation must stop. Failing to stop the interrogation makes anything the suspect said previously inadmissible in court. Some argue that the innocent do not fully exercise their Miranda rights, which could lead to a wrongful conviction (Lassiter & Pinegar, 2013).

Interventions

An intervention is a strategy designed and implemented to reduce or change a behavior perceived to be negative and increase a behavior perceived to be positive. In the criminal justice system, interventions are implemented to provide an individual with a support system and the knowledge, skills, and tools to modify their behavior. Those already engaging in criminal behavior and those at risk of engaging in such behavior can be targeted by interventions.

Programs and interventions should be designed and implemented to prevent those at risk of being radicalized into terrorism. Interventions should target individuals that exhibit a consistent pattern of criminal behavior (Committee of Ministers of the Council of Europe, 2000). These interventions should seek to protect and deter such individuals from engaging in criminal or terrorist behavior, and minimize vulnerabilities of them engaging in crime and terrorism (Committee of Ministers of the Council of Europe, 2000).

Additionally, while investigating a crime or an individual, law enforcement officials can choose to *intervene* with a suspect instead of, or in addition to, interviewing or interrogating them. In contrast to interviews and interrogations, interventions are nonaccusatory, nonconfrontational, and conversational in nature. For example, the interventionist can inquire if the suspect is provided with the legal support they need.

The conversational nature of intervening allows the interventionist to appeal and engage with a suspect on a more human-to-human level. This communication style may be something the suspect is not used to in a law enforcement setting, as being spoken to in a friendly manner where there are no labels of "authority" may put the suspect at ease and comfort. More information can be gathered from an individual if they are *spoken to*, instead of being constantly questioned, interviewed, interrogated, and reprimanded. As humans, we have a basic need to *belong* and be *accepted* by others, and having an interventionist can encourage the building of rapport and make the suspect feel like someone is putting in an effort to help, support, and understand their circumstances.

This conversational nature of interventions is appealing not only to the suspect but also to the interventionist. The greater the rapport with the interventionist, the more likely the suspect will be more open and communicative in providing the details of their involvement in a crime. An honest and communicative suspect in turn can improve and quicken the investigative process. Furthermore, the less formal and less structured nature of intervening makes it flexible and easy to engage in. The humanistic orientation of interventions enables ethical boundaries to be firmly kept in place, reducing the possibility of interventionists engaging in malpractice and mistreating suspects.

Based on the nature of the technique described above and on his own experiences, this author argues that the intervention technique is more useful in getting to know the terrorist, compared with interviews and interrogations. Adding to its appeal is the fact that compared with interviews and interrogations, intervening through program implementation can have a long-term effect on reducing rates of crime and terrorism.

However, interventions also have some drawbacks. Due to their subjective conversational nature, intervention techniques may be hard to generalize across countries and cultures. Some researchers (e.g., Banse et al., 2013) argue that there is not enough empirical evidence to demonstrate that interventions help reduce criminal behaviors from new and repeat offenders. Applying large-scale intervention programs can also be challenging as they require cooperation across various levels and departments, both inside and outside the criminal justice system (Committee of Ministers of the Council of Europe, 2000). See Table 7.1 for a summary of the differences among the techniques discussed.

Interview and Interrogation Techniques

There are a host of interrogation techniques published and used worldwide; however, some argue that the generalizability and applicability of these techniques is impaired as they have no scientific validity (Lassiter & Pinegar, 2013).

Reid Technique

The Reid technique, developed by John E. Reid & Associates, Inc., is used worldwide. It is a rigorous, structured, and popular interviewing and interrogation

Table 7.1   Summary of Differences between Interviews, Interrogations, and Interventions

Point of Difference	Interviews	Interrogations	Interventions
Process	Less formal and less structured	More formal and more structured	Less formal and less structured
Goal	Gather information	Elicit confession	Provide support and build rapport to enable gathering of information
Place of conduct	Anywhere	Law enforcement facility	Anywhere
Communication	Dialogue	Monologue	Dialogue
Communication majority	Interviewee	Interrogator	No majority
Tone	Generally nonaccusatory	Generally accusatory	Conversational
Note-taking	Occurs	Does not occur until confession	Can occur
Declaration of Miranda rights	Not required	Required if person taken into custody	Not required
Duration	Short; time limit	Can be long though not preferred; no time limit	Long-term through intervention programs

technique based on, what is argued as, culturally generalizable distinct facial emotional expressions as per Ekman's Facial Action Coding System.

It consists of three interrelated components, which include (John E. Reid & Associates, Inc., n.d.)

1. Factual analysis—The process of analyzing suspect-specific information (e.g., gender and ethnicity) and suspect–crime-related information (e.g., motive, opportunity, and ability) to ascertain an individual's probable guilt or innocence (Orlando, 2014).
2. Behavior analysis interview—The *nonaccusatory* process of questioning an individual in a way that evokes certain behaviors. The interviewer analyzes

and distinguishes between the person's "normal" and "abnormal" nonverbal behaviors and verbal answers in response to the *behavior-provoking* questions asked. This behavior analysis enables the interviewer to determine whether the person is telling the truth or lying.

3. Interrogation—The *accusatory* process, which occurs in monologue format, whereby an interrogator tries to elicit a confession from a potential suspect who, based on substantial evidence, appears to be guilty. The interrogator adopts a professional, patient, understanding, noncoercive, nonaggressive, and nonmanipulative approach.

The nine steps of interrogation for the interrogator include (Orlando, 2014; John E. Reid & Associates, Inc., n.d.)

1. Positive confrontation—Confronting the suspect with their probable guilt in light of substantial evidence.
2. Theme development—Presenting the suspect with a moral justification or *theme* to their crime.
3. Handling denials—Preventing the suspect from making denials of accusation. Guilty suspects are more likely to ask for permission to speak before denying an accusation, while those who are innocent are more likely to assert their innocence without asking for permission to speak—consistently and more progressively—with time.
4. Overcoming objections—Accepting claims of innocence. Guilty suspects are more likely to assert their innocence with an objection if accusations of denial prove unsuccessful. Objections may be emotional, factual, and/or moral. Instead of making objections, the innocent will continue to profess their innocence.
5. Procurement and retention of suspect's attention—Attaining and retaining the suspect's attention on the theme, and away from the consequences of a confession. The innocent do not generally reach this stage; hence, the following steps are generally directed toward the potentially guilty. Attention can be attained and retained by maintaining close physical distance with the suspect.
6. Handling the suspect's passive mood—Maintaining a consistent understanding, sympathetic approach toward the suspect who is likely to have begun to accept their guilty circumstances and as a result may be displaying a withdrawn, passive, defeated, regretful, or sad stance.
7. Presenting an alternative question—Incriminatingly questioning the suspect to encourage a *short, simple* admission or acknowledgment of guilt.
8. Having the suspect orally relate various details of the offense—Getting the suspect to orally recount their crime, thereafter which more questions to reconfirm any details may be asked.
9. Converting an oral confession to a written confession—Attaining a written confession that the suspect signs, if they are in agreement with it.

Critique of the Reid Technique

Some research has indicated that the behavior analysis interview component can indicate a potential/deceptive suspect with 83% accuracy (Lassiter & Pinegar, 2013). However, lie detection scholars have argued that such accuracy cannot be attained (Lassiter & Pinegar, 2013).

Leo (2013) and Moore and Fitzsimmons (2011) argue that the general signs of deception may be inaccurate and that cognitively as humans, we are unable to make judgments of potential guilt or innocence and deceit or honesty. For instance, suspects may appear guarded and reserved; however, this may not be because they are deceptive, but instead because they are scared and anxious as it is the first time they are undergoing an interview or interrogation.

The possibility of innocent people making false confessions during interrogations cannot be overlooked either. The things the interrogator says can cause an innocent suspect to believe they are guilty—termed as *internalized false confession* (Moore & Fitzsimmons, 2011). Additionally, misclassification and contamination may also lead to false confession (Gudjonsson, 2011; Leo & Drizin, 2010; Orlando, 2014).

There may be those who apply the Reid technique without fully adhering to the interrogative style that needs to be adopted in conjunction with the technique. An interrogation style characterized by intimidation, control, and coercion can distress an innocent suspect, leading to a false confession. Drawbacks of administering the Reid technique include its lengthiness, robustness, and repetitiveness, making it difficult and time-consuming to administer.

PEACE Method

Compared with the Reid technique, the PEACE method is a less accusatory and less confrontational interview and interrogation technique used extensively in England, New Zealand, and Denmark (Orlando, 2014). Initially, there is a monologue as suspects describe their version of the events to the investigators, who do not interrupt. Only after the suspect fully provides their recounting do investigators begin questioning the suspect.

Investigators are prohibited from psychologically manipulating a potential suspect during the interview and interrogation process (Meissner et al., 2012). Instead, investigators pay attention to the manner in which suspects recount their version of events.

It is believed that potentially guilty suspects are likely to lie more:

More suspect lies and fabrications ⟶ flawed thinking and verbal communication ⟶ more inconsistencies ⟶ more likely to be potentially guilty.

Compared with other techniques, the PEACE method does not focus on or allow psychological manipulations to elicit confessions from potentially guilty suspects. Instead, the PEACE method focuses on uncovering as much information as possible in order to approve or disapprove theories of who the potentially guilty suspect is.

The five components of the PEACE method (Orlando, 2014) are

1. Preparation and planning—Investigators engage in preparations for the interview and interrogation, ascertain the goals of the interviews, and ascertain the number and sequence of interviews to be conducted. A written interview plan is outlined that includes, but is not limited to, questions or topics to be addressed with potential suspects, such as visiting the crime scene.

2. Engage and explain—Investigators seek active engagement from the suspect. Such engagement may permit greater rapport building, which could enable the suspect to trust the investigator and truthfully reveal any and all details of their involvement in the crime. The investigator should also display that they are listening and paying attention to the suspect. The investigator should display full transparency to the suspect by explaining the regulations of the interview/interrogation process.

3. Account—The investigator should present simple-worded, broad-ended questions that evoke lengthy, descriptive answers, with as much detail as possible, from the suspect.

4. Closure—Upon conclusion of the interview, the investigator provides a brief recount of the suspect's version of the events. This permits the suspect to present any questions and address any issues they have with the recounting.

5. Evaluate—The investigator evaluates the suspect's potential guilt or innocence based on their answers and behaviors during the interview, in addition to the wider investigation and evidence.

Critique of the PEACE Method

The PEACE method is inflexible, long, and cumbersome to administer (Clarke & Milne, 2001). Allowing the suspect to recount their version of events without interruptions impairs the investigation process as the investigators might forget certain questions or clarifications they may have wanted to address. Additionally, because they are allowed to speak uninterrupted, some suspects may begin to feel like they hold the authority during the interrogation/interview process. This false sense of authority can lead to the suspect being disrespectful and resistant toward the investigator and the investigation process, impairing the latter.

All these processes of interviewing, interrogation, and intervention are workable. You, the administrator of the process, must be comfortable with the method to be applied. Also, testing the process that achieves the best rapport and gets the most information from the accused has to be wagered in the selection formula.

Chapter 8

Techniques of Intervention

It is important to distinguish among the various methods by which one maintains a dialogue with an individual engaging in terrorist-related activities. As previously discussed in Chapters 6 and 7, interviews are used when trying to determine whether the suspect, who is held under investigation, has committed the terrorist act. The process of the interview is to ask questions with the primary goal of information gathering. The goal of interrogation, much like interviewing, is that of eliciting information from the potential terrorist. However, unlike a simple question-and-answer format, interrogation involves the process of using various techniques, from rapport building to deception, to even the utilization of torture.

A third, yet uncommon method of dialoguing with a terrorist is through psychological and social intervention. While the person intervening may be able to gather data about the terrorist's life and history, this process has less to do with collecting information about the terror attack and more to do with creating change within the terrorist. Through intervention, the ultimate goal is to ensure that the detained terrorist will not be a future risk to the public.

So how might one go about rehabilitating terrorists? One such form of intervention involves the process of deradicalization, which aims to change the radical ideologies held by detained terrorists. Terrorists may go through certain processes that result in a reduced likelihood for future violence. Hence, it is important to clarify the distinctions between these processes—namely disengagement and deradicalization. *Disengagement* is the process by which the terrorist no longer engages with the terrorist group, although not necessarily breaking away from the ideologies held by the group. A terrorist may choose to disengage from a terrorist organization for a number of reasons:

- ◼ If there is a change in the group dynamics within the terrorist organization
- ◼ If the terrorist begins to experience negative sentiment by other group members
- ◼ If the group leader of the terrorist organization has been killed or captured
- ◼ If the terrorist becomes disillusioned with the political aims of the group
- ◼ If the goals of the terrorist have been achieved
- ◼ If the terrorist group has been suppressed by the state

In these circumstances, the terrorist is physically breaking away from the organization at large. However, if he still holds radical ideologies, he continues to pose a threat to public safety.

Deradicalization, on the other hand, is the process of intentionally changing the terrorist's radical ideologies by moving individuals away from extreme violence. The goal of deradicalization would be to eventually release the terrorist from detention. Rather than behavioral change through disengagement, deradicalization aims to create psychological change in ideology, thereby leading to the behavioral change (i.e., the individual no longer engaging in terrorist-related activity). It needs to be kept in mind that both processes may or may not occur together. Disengagement from the group does not necessarily change the person's radical views.

The process of deradicalization involves the deconstruction of factors that led the individual to become radicalized in the first place. The first part of the process involves distancing the detained terrorist from the extremist group. At this point in time, the terrorist is most likely placed in prison, making disengagement easier. If the terrorist has been sentenced to undergo deradicalization, he must be placed in a detention center, away from other members of his group so as to begin disengaging him from others holding similar extreme ideologies. It is possible that the individual may meet others in prison with similar ideologies; therefore, the individual's placement in the detention center is highly important in ensuring that he is truly disengaged from the group.

The second part of the process begins with changing the radical ideology the terrorist believes to be true. Many terrorists, particularly ethnogeographic political and religious terrorists, hold extreme ideologies based on scriptures and literary excerpts from religious or philosophical texts. Very often, specific passages from these texts are used to justify the terrorist's cause. Therefore, clerics and other facilitators who are knowledgeable of these literary texts should be involved in having discussions and debates with the terrorist over interpretations of them. It is important that these facilitators possess adequate knowledge of these texts, as well as maintain authority and respect by those who have been detained. When well-respected facilitators and moderators engage in dialogue with terrorists by providing trust and moral support, they are more likely to be successful in countering the radical ideologies of the terrorists (Ellie & Nur, 2015). Over time, these facilitators can be successful in changing extremist interpretations of a political or religious ideology. Additionally, it is important for practitioners of deradicalization programs to incorporate the cultural norms of the terrorist while maintaining these discussions. This approach was utilized by the Saudi Arabian government as part of a multi-pronged terrorist deradicalization program. By having clerics of the Islamic faith engage in an in-depth discussion of the Islamic text versus misinterpretations used by terrorist organizations, these facilitators served as mentors and built strong relationships with those in the program. In doing so, the Saudi Arabian government claims to have a success rate of 80–90% within their participants, with low recidivism (Bouchek, 2008).

Another aspect of the deradicalization process involves improving the quality of life for the terrorist. Quite often individuals become a part of terrorist organizations as a result of external factors, such as difficult socioeconomic conditions, as well as internal factors, including low levels of self-efficacy and self-esteem and challenges gaining control of their lives. Therefore, this aspect seeks to reduce potential economic barriers by providing educational opportunities, vocational training, and job placement. By being provided the opportunity to be a contributing member of society, the terrorist will experience an increase in self-worth and self-esteem. Terrorists can also be helpful in deradicalization efforts and researching the effectiveness of rehabilitation programs for other terrorists. This process allows released terrorists to reintegrate back into society.

A main strategy in the reintegration process is involving family members of the terrorist, as well as the communities that have been hurt by the terrorist's actions. As challenging as this might be, it is crucial to provide psychoeducation and counseling to family members and the community at large so that they are able to accept the terrorist back into society. Doing so can potentially reduce the recidivism rate of the terrorist rejoining his terrorist organization (Ellie & Nur, 2015). As part of their multipronged approach, the Saudi Arabian deradicalization program utilized family members of the terrorist to help with the reintegration process. In doing so, the program was highly effective in changing the ideology of a large portion of the participants in their program (Bouchek, 2008). If the individual feels a need for belongingness with his family and community, he is unlikely to rejoin his terrorist group.

In order for successful recidivism from terrorism, it is important that the deradicalization program be well funded and comprehensive, to include all aspects of the process, including psychological counseling, reeducation of extreme philosophies and religious beliefs, and the inclusion of the terrorist's family members and community in the process. In addition, the state must be able to provide incentives as positive reinforcement in keeping the terrorist away from the terrorist group. These incentives can come in the form of housing, monetary income, or education or through providing employment opportunities. In addition, when utilizing deradicalization programs, the state or government should track recidivism rates of terrorists who have been released from detention. This can be accomplished by having the participants of the program check in with a security agency on a regular basis. Successful intervention occurs when the terrorist is able to reintegrate with society at large, is accepted by his community, and is able to function in various psychosocial domains of his life, as he did previously before becoming radicalized. Additionally, he must possess new skills learned from the program (vocational as well as psychological), which help him maintain employment and be introspective and self-critical of previously held ideologies.

When utilizing intervention as an approach, a few things need to be kept in mind by practitioners of deradicalization:

1. Terrorists hold extreme ideologies, which vary across terrorist groups. Therefore, a one-size-fits-all approach is unlikely to be effective in changing the ideologies of terrorists. These programs need to be adapted to the individual, his ideological background, and the participating communities, taking into account all cultural contexts.

2. The process of deradicalization is only one aspect of counter-terrorism, and if utilized in insolation it will likely result in partial success. Family members and the community must be involved in creating positive change for the detainee.

3. Deradicalization programs need to track recidivism by monitoring or following up with released detainees. Having family members involved with the individual can be particularly helpful in keeping track of the terrorist and can serve as a protective factor against recidivism. Furthermore, these programs need to engage in future research to measure success rates and improve upon intervention techniques.

4. When terrorists are released from detention after engaging in the program, stigmatization can go a long way in helping the individual be accepted or rejected by his community. If rejected, the terrorist is likely to rejoin the terrorist organization, as this group can allow him to feel a sense of belongingness that he would need to survive. Therefore, deradicalization programs need to ensure that the community receives psychoeducation on the dangers of stigmatization and the effectiveness of community acceptance.

5. When releasing detainees to reintegrate back into society, states should be able to provide incentives. It is important for states to provide education to the community at large, who might view these incentives as "rewarding the terrorist." If states are able to get some buy-in from the community, they may be able to effectively provide the detainee with these basic needs.

Currently, while some countries have discussed the success of these interventions, there has not been sufficient data to indicate their efficacy within the terrorist population. This is not to say that intervention does not work. The limited available research has suggested that deradicalization has shown some signs of success in reducing the rates of terrorist offenses. This calls for future research to examine the efficacy of interventions in reducing recidivism within terrorist groups.

Best Process to Use

To know thy self is to understand your strengths and weaknesses. Then you can better relate to "the other." The result of your desired technique helps you realize your habits and your own personality characteristics, as these will determine the destiny of the aims at hand.

The method of intercession works best for this professional in the procedure that is "second nature"; the one that does not require slowed deliberation of thought and emotions when trying to impress with "the right question."

The strategy that establishes a nonthreatening rapport.

The method that makes you a better interviewer, interrogator, or intervener. This is the one in which you can pay attention and then your thoughts turn into words to follow the content flow.

The system that allows you to be comfortably flexible and spontaneous if appropriate.

Learning to be flexible with your style to accommodate the other. If one gets stuck in one process and learns nothing else, then they limit the scope of communication and understanding. How can you gain cooperation when there is no sense of connectedness? Even when in disagreement, there needs to be collaboration.

Current Research and Critique on Interview, Interrogation, and Intervention Techniques: Critique of Coercive Interview, Interrogation Techniques

Research has found that in general, individuals believe and report coercive accusatory confession-seeking interrogation and interview techniques as less acceptable, less effective and less ethically conscious (Jones & Brimbal, 2017). Interestingly, Jones and Brimbal (2017) found that adoption of coercive accusatory confession-seeking interrogation techniques is influenced by individual differences in beliefs on authoritarianism and "belief in a just world." The results revealed that compared with other participants, participants whose reported scores were high on these measures found coercive accusatory confession-seeking interrogation techniques more acceptable (Jones & Brimbal, 2017).

Based on this finding, this author argues that while there may be legalized prohibitions of coercive accusatory interrogation techniques due to ethical reasons, interrogators may still be inclined to directly adopting or indirectly displaying behaviors inherent in such techniques, dependent on their intrinsic views of the world. Therefore, this author recommends that tests should be administered to measure whether law enforcement interrogators are high on these traits and if they are, then measures should be taken to ensure these individual differences and intrinsic biases do not influence the interrogation process and the adoption of certain interrogation techniques.

While multiple countries and governments worldwide have explicitly banned the usage of torture techniques and prohibited the usage of coercive interrogative practices, some interrogators still employ these *enhanced* techniques that can be perceived as harsh and psychologically manipulative, while blurring ethical and legal boundaries. Employment of harsh *enhanced* interrogation techniques does not guarantee accurate information extraction from the suspect. This is because the usage of such techniques dehumanizes the suspect, argues this author and researchers like Alison and Alison (2017).

While our perceptions about how we are treated is subjective, generally and psychologically speaking, as humans we like to treat others the way we are treated. By applying this logic, one could argue that the dehumanizing aspect inherent in harsh *enhanced* interrogative practices could lead the suspect to develop a negative attitude toward the interrogator and the interrogation process. The development of negative attitudes could reduce the suspect's cooperation with the interrogator as the suspect may be more resistant and less willing to answer the interrogator's questions about the crime.

When dehumanized, we feel powerless. The interrogator or detainer assumes a position of power and authority and is perceived as being in full control of the suspect (Alison & Alison, 2017). In an attempt to reclaim some of this power and authority, the suspect may try to purposely say things that may challenge the interrogator and the interrogation process. For example U.S.—the purposeful provision of inaccurate information. Consequently, harsh '*enhanced*' interrogative techniques, could further psychologically and cognitively distance the suspect from the interrogator and could impair the quality and outcome of the interrogation process.

The wider literature is critical of the efficacy of harsh '*enhanced*' interrogation practices (Alison & Alison, 2017; Jones & Brimbal, 2017). Some argue that these techniques are employed not to impair the psychological well-being of the suspect, but for the interrogator to establish control and authority during the interrogation process (Alison & Alison, 2017). However, such reasoning is inaccurate as the psychological well-being of the suspect *is* impacted. Research (O'Mara, 2015; Morgan et al., 2013; Alison & Alison, 2017) has shown that the suspect's brain is under immense duress when such practices are employed, which diminishes their recall, impairing the quality and output of the overall interrogative process.

It is also important to note that when dealing with accused terrorists, the efficiency of employing coercive, harsh or psychologically manipulative interrogative techniques is questionable as upon recruitment to a terrorist group, most terrorists may have undergone psychological *resistance training* to prevent the "leakage" of valuable information to legal authorities, if they are captured or brought to justice.

Research has shown that interviews and interrogations have the potential to be more effective when they focus on information gathering and adopt a non-accusatorial stance compared to seeking confessions and adopting an accusatorial stance (Russano et al., 2014; Evans et al., 2013; Moston & Engelberg, 2011; Hartwig et al., 2005; Alison & Alison 2017).

Chapter 9

Understanding Terrorist Attacks: Methods, Mode, Tactics, and Strategies

Terrorism is the kind of warfare that never tries to solve an actual conflict. Terrorist methods are usually used when dealing with unresolved political issues that impact a large number of people. This violent and aggressive form of warfare has been used many times throughout history, and has been aimed at territory acquisition and dominance, the building of sovereign states, and the overthrowing of an existing government. Aside from the political motives of terrorism, terrorist activities were also used to economically deprive a certain group, or establish supremacy and dominance over them (Madigan, 2017).

Terrorist attacks are always created to incite fear and the maximum amount of publicity. They also implant a constant fear that such attacks would escalate to include the use of weapons of mass destruction. Terrorist organizations and factions invest a vast amount of premeditation to carefully plan their attacks, and they train their participants in the same means to which an army would train a soldier. A majority of their funding is received through organized crime and arms deals within the arms industry. They take great advantage of "new" communication devices, as well as trusted foot soldiers and couriers. From this evolves another terrorist tactic, cyber terrorism, where they use electronic devices to further their agenda. Examples of this include threats made by phone, website defacing, and computer hacking.

There is enough evidence to suggest that the intent of terrorist groups is to commit acts of violence in order to

- Create a heightened sense of fear and moral panic
- Obtain local and/or global attention via mass media
- Instigate governments to resort to violence in order to be perceived as oppressive
- Engage in theft or extortion of money and/or weaponry for their group
- Destroy communication and public facilities to destroy the broader economic structure and have governments perceived as weak
- Attempt to influence governmental decisions
- Aim for the release of specific prisoners or captives
- Aim to retaliate and/or satisfy their sense of vengeance
- Attempt to reverse a guerrilla war through attacking major cities as a deflection in order for governments to counteract as they maintain control over their rural areas

Terrorism has become an unfortunate part of the modern world. Certain groups of people have begun to rely on violence to promote the change they crave, be it religious, political, or social. There seems to be a lot of isolated incidents, but it also seems that the threat of violence has become a common language. Violence has become a means to an end, which is all in all a very perverse idea.

Violent intentions of terrorists are translated into terrorist attacks, which can be divided into two categories: simultaneous attacks and single attacks (Deloughery, 2013).

Simultaneous attacks involve a series of subsequently occurring attacks, or attacks in two or more locations at the same time. These attacks require careful planning, coordination, training, and an increased input of financial and human resources. Due to the carefully planned nature of these attacks, they often cause a higher number of casualties, incite increased fear, and have a widespread impact (Deloughery, 2013). Such attacks are usually planned by the organization itself, and involve highly trained fighters aiming to maximize the impact of the attack. These attacks get a lot more media coverage, and hence inspire other attacks by terrorist sympathizers (Jetter, 2017).

Single attacks are single-incident attacks carried out by the terrorist organization or its sympathizers. These attacks may be planned or carried out on impulse. They have a smaller impact than coordinated attacks, and require lesser input of financial and human resources.

Research by Nesser and Stenersen (2014) provides insight into methods terrorists use during terrorist attacks. Simultaneous and single attacks involve the use of weapons, mass casualty bombings, hostage situations, and crude killing. Improvised explosive devices (IEDs) and homemade explosives (HMEs) are commonly used to maximize the number of fatalities. These explosives have been used by many terrorist organizations, including Al Qaeda, the Islamic State of Iraq and the Levant (ISIL), the Armed Islamic Group (GIA), and "lone-wolf" terrorists by concentrating chlorate mixtures, peroxide-based mixtures, and other high-grade explosives in pressure cookers, gas canisters, or cylinders. The majority of explosive devices are used for land-based attacks, while there have also been a few documented cases of air- and sea-based bombing plots.

There has also been an increase in the use of knives and firearms over the past decade. Research shows that the use of knives, guns, and rifles has increased by 33% in the past decade (Nesser & Stenersen, 2014).

Single-Actor Terrorism

In recent years, there has been a rise in single-incident attacks carried out by terrorist sympathizers. These attacks have become possible due to social media and technology as these platforms enable terrorist organizations to have an international following base. Moreover, recruiting terrorists online makes it easier for terrorist recruiters to remain anonymous, and avoid detection by law enforcement agencies. It is interesting to note that while sympathizers are often lone-wolf terrorists, they rarely act alone, as demonstrated in 60% of the attacks in the past decade (Nesser & Stenersen, 2014). This is evident in past terrorist acts, such as the Orlando nightclub shooting (Goldman & Blinder, 2017), the 2015 San Bernardino attacks, and the 2017 Manchester suicide bombing, in which the attacks were carried out either by a pair or by the attacker who was supported by a spouse, friend, or kindred relative.

Suicide Terrorism

Suicide violence is also a growing trend seen in various terrorist organizations. To carry out a suicide mission, terrorist groups hire individuals who may be inherently suicidal or who are suicidal because of past trauma, or train young men to believe their fantasized version of "martyrdom" (Speckhard & Yayla, 2015). While the attacker has suicidal intentions in most cases, there have also been instances where they are unaware of the suicidal nature of the mission, and are tricked into accepting the mission by the terrorist organization (Al-Qaisi, 2011). Similarly, animals have also been used for such missions (AFP, 2010). While suicide missions are usually done using explosives, attackers have also been known to use guns and rifles. These mass shootings are done with the intent of shooting oneself once the shooter has caused fatalities, or by being shot by law enforcement officials (Lankford, 2011). If the attacker does not have access to bombs or guns, they may resort to plowing vehicles into crowded areas—a mode of attack that has become increasingly popular in recent years.

With the recent rise in suicide terrorism, it is important to understand the reasons behind the increasing preference of this mode of attack by terrorist organizations.

Research by Corte and Giménez-Salinas (2009) shows that suicide terrorism has certain advantages over other modes of attack, including

- Highly destructive and lethal impact: The damage caused by suicide terrorism in terms of fatalities surpasses that of other methods of terrorist attacks. Moreover, as the attacker is keen on attaining martyrdom, he may employ the most lethal ways of attack without having to fear for his own safety.
- Simplification of attack process: As suicide attacks are usually carried out by lone attackers, the attacker can adapt to sudden changes and avoid having to rely on others for instructions.
- Widespread media coverage: These attacks are extensively covered by the media, and generate mass fear, hopelessness, and social disturbance among people. Moreover, suicide attacks receive significantly more media coverage than any other type of terrorist attack (Jetter, 2014). Hence, terrorists may resort to suicide missions to have a widespread impact and generate mass hysteria and fear.

Chemical Attacks

These attacks involve the dispersal of toxic industrial and commercial chemicals, as well as chemicals produced biologically. Chemicals such as sarin, botulinum toxin, saxitoxin, chloropicrin, and ricin are released into the environment, with the aim to cause fatalities through inhalation and direct contact. These toxins can be released directly into the environment in food and water supplies or in ventilation systems of buildings, and by use of explosive devices (Department of Homeland Security, n.d.). The effects of such attacks can be disastrous, ranging from irritation, nausea, and seizures to death. While chemical attacks by terrorists are uncommon, they are not unheard of. Terrorist organizations such as Al Qaeda have used chlorine contained in explosive tankers and trucks, causing injuries, illness, and fatalities (Multi-National Corps, 2007).

Radiological Dispersal Device

A radiological dispersal device (RDD) or a *dirty bomb* is a weapon of mass destruction, combining explosives with radioactive materials. Dispersal may also be done by releasing powdered or aerosolized forms of radioactive materials in public places. While RDDs may not be fatal, they are intended to cause contamination of areas, have a psychological impact on civilians, and increase the risk of cancer (Davis et al., 2003). Terrorist organizations are suspected to have acquired radioactive material, but they have not launched a widespread attack using RDDs. In 2002, a terrorist linked to Al Qaeda was accused of planning to detonate a dirty bomb

(Ripley, 2002). Similarly, Islamic State of Iraq and Syria (ISIS) militants acquired uranium compounds from Mosul University, but they were unable to launch an attack as it was unenriched (Chiaramonte, 2014).

Biological Attacks

Biological attacks involve the use of infectious agents, pathogens, and biological toxins to infect, harm, and kill people, animals, and plants. These weapons are easy to produce and are cheaper than conventional weapons, hence making them appealing to terrorists (U.S. Commission on National Security, 1999). Moreover, contamination and contact with biotoxic agents can remain undetected for long periods of time, making it difficult for healthcare professionals to minimize the damage caused. Biological attacks have been used throughout history, with weapons including plague, smallpox, and measles. However, there has been an increase in the use of anthrax, Ebola virus, botulinum toxin, and cultures of *Shigella dysenteriae* in the 1990s (SIU School of Medicine, n.d.). Contemporary terrorist organizations such as ISIL and Al Qaeda have been known to plan biological attacks using ricin and cyanide, and have employed chemists to train fighters in biological warfare (Mowatt-Larsen, 2010).

Uncertain is the correlation between
personality profile, terrorist type,
and the selection of weapons to be
used in actions of terror.

Effects of Mass Media on Terrorism

In today's world, with the rapid development of technology, traditional media has evolved and expanded to include the Internet. We get notifications and news alerts instantly, in real time, on our mobile devices, laptops, and computers much before these stories are even covered in other forms of media, such as newspapers. Although benefits such as quick access, spread of current information, and increased awareness are facilitated by the media, this comes with a heavy price.

The 9/11 attacks in New York, the 26/11 attacks in Mumbai, and the Madrid and London bombings are some of the many terrorist attacks covered extensively in the media. Media exposure is a goal of many terrorist groups. Attracting the audience's attention is important to terrorist groups who value the media as they offer a direct outlet for them to attract this attention and get their message across, for free. This is, to some, pure exploitation of the media outlets (Wilkinson, 1997).

Some believe that the media has given terrorists a voice and that terrorism is almost a symptom and somewhat of a brainchild of the media. Margaret Thatcher called publicity "the oxygen of terrorism" (Apple, 1985). Paul Watson thinks that the media is somewhat responsible for the increasing number of terrorists and terror attacks, and states that the terrorists use the media as the sole means of delivering information to the public. Interestingly, Paul Watson's organization Sea Shepherd Conservation Society, involves a vessel that takes direct action against whaling ships and attempts to sabotage them, has been labeled an ecoterrorist. However, the organization has not claimed any casualties yet.

Though there have been efforts made by the media to censor certain people or organizations that carry out terrorism in hopes of prevention, this may in fact act to further exasperate the situation and cause unheard of or suppressed terrorists to become even more violent and attract the attention they desire. The Weather Underground is a good example of how an organization, while causing no casualties, did not get any media attention until they succumbed to using terrorist acts. The media remains the largest outlet for terrorists today.

The media is motivated to get information out there as quickly as possible. Many times, this haste can lead to the public being misinformed due to the reporting of inaccurate, unverified material and the spreading of false information. For example, popular media publications have been quick to label acts of violence as "terrorism" when they are not. The media, in their tone and descriptions, also stereotype certain types of individuals as terrorists when in reality, they are not terrorists. Some argue that the media has played a huge role in the spread of Islamophobia. To the dismay of many, the media also "protects" individuals who are terrorists, by portraying them in a way that defends their acts of terrorism—for example, by attributing their motivations to mental health issues even though this may be inaccurate.

Some argue that the media also overexaggerates and overreacts to terrorist events. The "terrorism industry" includes, but is not limited to, the media, politicians, and security firms (Mueller, 2005). Terrorism "sells" and overexaggerating and overreacting to threats serve the media's commercial interests and politicians' political interests, while also offering them reputational gains and elevating their status (Mueller, 2005). Should the overreaction and overexaggeration be proven to be true, politicians receive credit and their public approval ratings and the public's support for policies and government parties may soar. For example, Thórisdóttir and Jost (2011) showed that the greater the threat, such as a terrorist attack, the greater the number of conservative attitudes and higher affiliations shown toward the Republican Party.

Dr. Louise Richardson, a world-renowned terrorism expert, said that the U.S. government and media reaction to 9/11 was an overreaction as it was something that they had not experienced before (Ward, 2015). This begs the question of whether that "new experience" and "overreaction" provoked decades of subsequent overreactions by the media and a cycle of retaliatory attacks by the government and terrorist groups. Kydd and Walter (2006) refer to a "provocation strategy" that terrorists employ, intended to provoke a violent reaction from the government "enemy" in response to acts of terrorism, which ends up mobilizing support by radicalizing the masses. The media, with its international coverage, provides this platform and yet again helps terrorists attain one more of their goals.

People vulnerable to terrorism are the most at risk of being radicalized. Retaliation attacks by the government extensively covered in the media can create terrorist sympathizers and further polarize society—a goal of many terrorists. This is because the media romanticizes terrorists as "heroes." A famous quote illustrating this is "One man's terrorist is another man's freedom fighter." In the wake of the Rouen attack, French publications like *Le Monde* and *La Croix* acknowledged that the media has a tremendous role to play in the fight against terrorism, which is not just limited to governments, law enforcement, and intelligence services, and they announced that they would stop publishing content that "glorifies" and romanticizes terrorists (Fenoglio, 2016). This author also believes that we should assume greater responsibility in preventing the publishing of content and spreading of information that glorifies and aids terrorists and their causes.

Media coverage of live terrorist attacks can also increase the complexity of security operations, compromising the lives, success, and response of security forces. For example, terrorist groups may be watching this live coverage and communicating with their members on the ground, helping them evade capture. Media sources may continually replay graphic content, leading to consistent panic, fear, and anxiety much after the terrorist attack, in order to increase their TRP ratings and for purely commercial reasons, to the detriment of national interest, national security, and the psychological well-being of society. Mueller (2005) refers to this as "fear-mongering," which the terrorism industry benefits from. Presidential speeches by George W. Bush and Tony Blair contained a high proportion of fear and anger-arousing content (DeCastella & McGarty, 2011). This reveals that "emotional appeals" and fear-mongering tactics are strategically used to garner more public support in favor of certain counter-terrorism policies.

Emotions aroused by the media and politicians (terrorism industry) to support counter-terrorism policies include (Iyer, et al., 2014):

- Fear (reduce or remove terrorist threat) $\longrightarrow$ policies of negotiation and protection from future threats and attacks
- Sympathy (helping and giving) $\longrightarrow$ policies that support victims of terrorism
- Anger (challenging the perpetrators) $\longrightarrow$ aggressive policies to fight terrorism

The "dread risk" hypothesis postulated by Gigerenzer (2006) theorizes that less probable and high-damage eventualities, such as terrorist attacks, cause more fear in individuals. López-Rousseau (2005) found that after the 2004 Madrid train bombings, Spaniards reduced their rail and road travels to avoid the dread risk of a terror attack. In a similar vein, Gigerenzer's (2006) research found that for 1 year after 9/11, Americans reduced air travel and increased their road travel, providing more evidence for the dread risk theory. These studies show the huge impact terrorism has on psychological well-being as revealed by this dread risk–motivated decision making.

Engaging in terrorism and causing widespread negative emotions in the public is psychological warfare (Horgan, 2014), and the media catalyzes this through their content. This is also another goal of terrorist groups, which the media helps attain. The media uses emotionally arousing content, images, and videos to maintain and attract audiences (Gadarian, 2010). Different emotions are evoked depending on what content is used. Published images of victims evoke sympathy, while images of perpetrators evoke fear and anger (Iyer et al., 2014).

Competition exists between types of mass media; for example, during the 9/11 attacks, members of the public were highly more likely to watch the news on TV, rather than read the news from the newspaper (Gadarian, 2010). This could be due to the emotionally arousing video content that can be displayed on news channels and not through print media. There has been widespread debate about what sort of content the media should display as the media holds a much bigger responsibility than just covering stories and events. What is portrayed in mass media influences our perceptions, opinions, attitudes, and behaviors on a host of things, including terrorism.

Young children watch this gruesome coverage of terrorist attacks, which scars their minds and lives forever. Some would argue that such content is far too graphic for young children to view; just as an R-rated movie restricts the age of audience members for a particular movie, this author wonders whether it is appropriate for news channels to display such content that is easily accessible to young children? Even if the television and news channels restrict the display of certain graphic content, the Internet has far less restrictions, and it is very easy for young children, if not monitored, to "stumble" across inappropriate content, to the delight of terrorists. Additionally, anonymization makes the Internet alluring and provides a breeding ground for terrorists to communicate with individuals at risk of being radicalized, allowing opportunities for the latter to address their questions to terrorists and strengthen their pro-terrorism attitudes and behaviors.

A multitude of studies have shown how terrorist groups recruit and radicalize potential members through Internet chatrooms (Kaplan, 2006). The comments sections on websites covering terrorism news reveal a divided world and provide easy access for terrorist groups to leverage their resources to mobilize more support for their cause by spreading propaganda and receiving funds. Terrorist group manifestos are easily available online for the public to access. Terrorist groups have websites that provide information in detail about their cause and how to become a member.

Terrorist groups have Twitter accounts (Murgia, 2017), post videos on YouTube, and have an active social media presence. The millions and billions of accounts present on social media websites provide a huge pool of potential "candidates" for terrorists to recruit. When a social media application blocks one terrorist account, ten more open. This makes it hard for companies like Twitter and Facebook to monitor and control terrorist "infiltration" into their social media outlets and protect their online communities. Furthermore, there is plenty of information available online that indirectly radicalizes members of the public. For example, there is detailed step-by-step information available online on how to build bombs, which could potentially inspire lone-wolf acts of terrorism.

Not only does the Internet offer members of the public with access to information that enables them to build weapons of mass destruction, but also terrorist groups have access to deadly weapons through the "dark web." The dark web is also known as the "invisible web," the "deep web," and the "deep net," referring to the deeper layers of the Internet that are not easily accessible via traditional, regular search engines (Weimann, 2016). Self-radicalized individuals access weapons via the dark web, to commit lone-wolf acts of terrorism in countries with rigorous security controls (Maxey, 2018).

Maxey (2018) found that terrorist groups and self-radicalized individuals are using the dark web's "crypto-bazaars," social media channels, and e-commerce sites to access deadly military equipment that is far from traditional. This author argues that the mere accessibility of deadly nontraditional weapons to terrorist groups and individuals via the dark web makes the Internet all the more dangerous and potentially catastrophic to the lives of many.

Fischer et al. (2011) found that of the short articles that did not publish terror-related pictures versus those that did versus articles that published both pictures and terrorist motives, the first two conditions (articles with no pictures and articles with pictures and motives) aroused less negative emotions and protected the psychological well-being of the public. This author thus argues that the media has a responsibility to publish content that protects the psychological well-being of society and does not impair it.

This author believes that similarly, other negative effects of the media can be curbed, if efforts are made and committed to by all employees, media firms, and governments worldwide to ensure that

- Accurate, verified information is conveyed, even if it costs a firm the privilege of being the first to cover the story
- The public is informed of false information, even if it was released by the same media firm
- Those who willingly publish false information while aware of the consequences are apprehended
- Online censorship is increased
- Publishing content which "glorifies" terrorism and "romanticizes" terrorists is banned
- Investigative journalism is encouraged
- Content, especially graphic content, is displayed carefully and responsibly, even at the cost of viewership numbers and TRP ratings

The Efficacy of Rapport-Based Intervention Techniques

Comparatively, research has shown that the usage of rapport-based methods, to extract information from a suspect, has greater efficacy (Alison & Alison, 2017). This author argues that the intervention technique is one such *rapport-building method* which has the capacity and potential, depending on how it is used, to be an efficient technique of extracting information from a suspect. Interventions have a *humanistic appeal* enhancing the rapport-building process between the suspect and the intervenor and allowing the suspect to: develop a more favorable view of the intervenor (MacDonald et al., 2017), relate to and be more willing to share information with the intervenor.

Employing rapport-building methods is a popular intervention technique which is *flexible* and *can also be used while conducting interviews and interrogations*. Through the usage of interpersonal skills (Alison & Alison, 2017), rapport-building methods, as the name suggests, facilitate the creation of a good rapport, cooperation and communication between the rapport-builder and the suspect. Empirically however, it is important to note that defining, measuring and studying rapport is challenging due to the multiple elements and factors that influence rapport building (e.g., culture) and the confidential nature of interviews, interrogations and interventions.

David Petraeus, a former CIA Director and U.S. Army general officer was quoted saying "the best way for an interrogator to extract information is to become his best friend" (Clark, 2014; Alison & Alison, 2017). While critics may argue that this statement is overly simplistic, what it alludes to is central to the humanistic-based rapport-building process; and that is treating the accused as an equal with respect and dignity as you would treat your friend.

For example, something as small as addressing the suspect as the *"accused"* rather than the *"suspect"* is a practice this author employs when *intervening with* individuals accused of a crime. Based on his experiences, this author argues that paying attention to *how we intervene* with rather than *question or interrogate* the *accused*, in addition to subtle non-behavioral cues such as our body language, tone of voice and eye contact, has an impact on the rapport-building process and the quality of information gathered.

The most commonly reported effective rapport-building methods include self-disclosure, sympathy or empathy and finding mutual agreements (Vallano et al., 2015). Exercising patience, tolerance, and self-control are believed to be critical to the rapport-building process (U.S. Army Field Manual, 2006).

It is natural to perceive rapport building, display empathy and other positive interpersonal relations, with suspects accused of terrorism, as emotionally challenging. Regardless of how heinous the crime, this author argues that law enforcement officials should uphold and tailor their behavior toward the accused as per the defining principle of the criminal justice system—"innocent until proven guilty."

Additionally, using rapport-building techniques not only enhances the quality of the information received from the suspect, but also the timing of such information disclosure; the greater the rapport, the faster the information disclosure during the interview and/or interrogation (Goodman-Delahunty et al., 2014; Alison & Alison, 2017).

The justice process is also influenced by rapport-based information-gathering approaches as Meissner et al. (2014) demonstrated that the usage of such approaches decreases the likelihood of attaining false confessions. This is because in comparison, accusatory, coercive confession-seeking approaches cause significant duress and distress, evoke fear and anxiety and impair the psychological well-being of suspects. Such suspects, although innocent, may be inclined to make a false confession so that they can put an end to the psychological torture, manipulation, and coercion.

Analysis of an Intervention Technique and Suggestions to Enhance the Quality of Information Gathering

In tandem with Alison and Alison (2017), this author argues that information-gathering is positively associated with adaptive, humanistic, rapport-based intervention approaches and negatively associated with maladaptive, dehumanizing, coercive, and accusatory-based approaches.

Alison et al. (2013) created the ORBIT coding framework—Observing Rapport-Based Interpersonal Techniques. Through ORBIT, video recordings of suspect–interrogator interactions were studied, measured, coded, and organized into two categories—adaptive (enabling communication) and maladaptive (deterring communication) (Alison et al., 2013). ORBIT research has focused on studying individuals convicted of committing acts of terrorism (Alison & Alison, 2017). ORBIT studies have found that rapport-based approaches led to more positive communication interactions, suspect cooperation and the disclosure of critical information such as motive and opportunity (Alison et al., 2013). ORBIT studies found that even the slightest expression of any maladaptive communication led to lower suspect cooperation and impaired information gathering.

Alison and Alison (2017) also argue that the stance adopted by the interrogator/interviewer/intervener at the start of the information-gathering process influences the quality and output of the entire process. Consistency is key however at various stages of the information-gathering process, different interpersonal skills may be better suited; the usage of the interpersonal skill and timing of its execution is influential to the process in its entirety and dependent on the information-gatherer's discretion. Therefore, the flexibility, adaptability, and versatility of the information-gatherer's repertoire of interpersonal skills is also stressed (Figure 9.1).

This author echoes the sentiment of Alison and Alison (2017) who argue that the first step to a more effective information-gathering process is not the adoption

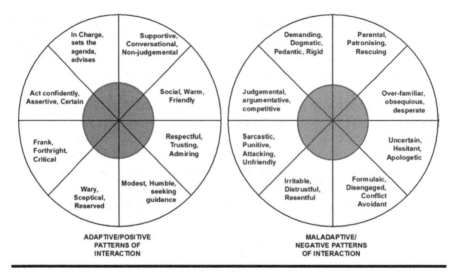

Figure 9.1 Adaptive and maladaptive variants of interpersonal behavior (Alison, L., & Alison, E. (2017). Revenge versus rapport: Interrogation, terrorism, and torture. *American Psychologist*, 72(3), 266).

of positive interpersonal skills and the employment of rapport-based techniques, but rather an intrinsic understanding—and execution—of the need to remove maladaptive, harsh, coercive, accusatory, and dehumanizing techniques.

According to recent research, there is a tendency for people to view coercive accusatory confession-seeking interrogation techniques as less acceptable, less effective and less ethically-conscious (Jones & Brimbal, 2017). Interestingly, the researchers of this study found that adoption of coercive accusatory confession-seeking interrogation techniques is influenced by individual differences in beliefs on authoritarianism and "belief in a just world". The results revealed that compared with others, participants whose reported scores were high on these measures found coercive accusatory confession-seeking interrogation techniques more acceptable.

Based on this finding, this author argues that while there may be legalized prohibitions of coercive accusatory interrogation techniques due to ethical reasons, interrogators may still be inclined to directly adopting or indirectly displaying behaviors inherent in such techniques, dependent on their intrinsic views of the world. Therefore, this author recommends that tests should be administered to measure whether law enforcement interrogators are high on these traits and if they are, then measures should be taken to ensure these individual differences and intrinsic biases do not influence the interrogation process and the adoption of certain interrogation techniques.

Chapter 10

Track I: Profiling and Counter-Terrorism

Earlier definitions of *counter-terrorism* involved the tactics, techniques, and strategies used by governments, state militaries, and other agencies of law enforcement as a response to terrorist-related activities that are real or threatened. Typically, counter-terrorism efforts are twofold: the first efforts involve methods of prevention against terror attacks, while the second ones are measures taken during the event of a terror-related attack. Prevention methods include increasing surveillance, such as using cameras in public areas or having intelligence agencies closely monitor the Internet activity of possible suspects; placing security at public locations or events; and having stricter security checks across borders. Prevention methods could also include increasing and sharing intelligence across agencies. Counter-terrorist measures following a terrorist attack would include reactive military action, arrests, interrogations for information, and convictions.

Governments typically respond to terrorism in the above-mentioned ways. Unfortunately, depending on the political or social climate within a state, some counter-terrorism measures are adopted that may prove to be more harmful than helpful. These methods of counter-terrorism, such as interrogation techniques, as extensively discussed in Chapter 7, often do not make positive contributions to the goals of counter-terrorism, that is, reducing terrorist attacks. This is particularly true of interrogations that resort to using physical and psychological torture, resulting in the suspect providing incorrect information.

Furthermore, certain counter-terrorist measures that utilize aggressive policing tactics, such as profiling individuals based on race or religion, and discriminatory interrogations, grossly overstep human rights. Kruglanski and colleagues

(2007) found that not only do such measures violate human rights, but they also fail to support the goals of counter-terrorism as these tactics increase discriminatory attitudes between groups and have a tendency to polarize and alienate members of minority groups from society. Previous research has suggested that post–9/11, Muslims have reported feeling targeted and alienated due to them being racially profiled and discriminated when they are publicly questioned by authorities. Furthermore, questions such as "How many times do you pray?" and "Which mosque do you attend?" were viewed as attacking their religion as they appeared to have little to do with terrorism involvement. Such line of questioning can be considered a poor counter-terrorism attempt as they are likely to anger and isolate group members from society at large (Choudhury & Fenwick, 2011). In addition, members from a targeted group will be less willing to report terrorism-related activities, particularly if they perceive law enforcement as an untrustworthy authority (Blackwood, Hopkins, & Reicher, 2013; Tyler, Schulhofer, & Huq, 2010). Although security measures have greatly increased over the past few years, there has been no research to indicate that such counter-terrorist measures have had any impact in reducing the number of terrorist attacks occurring.

Therefore, when questioning individuals in the community of possible terrorist activity, it is recommended that law enforcement individuals do not focus their line of questioning on the individual's cultural or religious background. It is recommended that governing bodies provide their staff various trainings in diversity and culturally related issues that allow them to ask questions of possible terror-related activity without conflating these with a specific cultural or religious group. Furthermore, it is recommended that individuals within law enforcement form positive relationships with people in the community, rather than alienate certain groups from society. Not only does this narrow the gap between minorities and targeted groups from the public, but also it keeps the lines of communication open between the community and law enforcement, leading to better information gathering of possible terrorist-related activity.

However, while the above recommendations pertain to government agencies in their defenses against terrorism, the rest of this chapter focuses on counter-terrorism measures that individuals within the public can engage in. From a psychological perspective, the term *counter-terrorism* has evolved into targeting the radical ideology held by the terrorist group, rather than targeting the people or community holding these rigid ideologies. More specifically referred to as "psychological counterterrorism" (Everly, 2003, 57–59), these measures include:

- Preventing potentially radicalized individuals from joining terrorist groups
- Creating disagreement between members of a terrorist group
- Facilitating the exit of an individual from the group
- Reducing an individual's support for the group

As discussed in Chapter 8, "deradicalization programs" have been developed by other countries, including Yemen, Malaysia, Singapore, and Saudi Arabia. Typically, these programs work toward reversing the effects of the radicalization process on individuals, thereby reducing the chances of the person further engaging in acts of terrorism. However, deradicalization programs are typically provided to people who have been captured and convicted by the authorities of the state after being caught engaging in a terrorist-related activity. Needless to say, these programs are offered to radicalized individuals after the crime has already been committed. Yet radicalization itself is a process where the person being radicalized develops a mind-set that tends to become more extreme over time, a process that could take years to develop. It only makes sense that while deradicalization programs are offered to individuals who have been completely radicalized, there are other opportunities to intervene during different phases of the radicalization process. Therefore, it is important to distinguish between the types of interventions or preventative measures in terms of their goals and the phase of radicalization that the counter-terrorism measure is best suited for. Clutterback (2015) has indicated that there are three psychological counter-terrorism measures that can be utilized to reduce the spread of extremist ideology:

■ Deradicalization
■ Counterradicalization
■ Antiradicalization

As discussed in detail earlier in this text, deradicalization programs are those offered by state authorities to those already convicted of engaging in terrorist-related crimes. These individuals are those who would have completed the radicalization process, currently hold extreme ideology, and likely believe that violent behaviors are the solution for change. These individuals are those that pose a high risk to society as they have already engaged in terror-related crimes. Deradicalization programs would focus on rehabilitating the individual with the hopes of reducing their risk of violence and reintegrating them back into society in the future.

The second approach, counterradicalization, can be targeted toward individuals who are currently in the process of being radicalized. At this point in time, the individual is likely exhibiting some behavioral changes, may begin to engage in violent behaviors, and is likely spending much of their time focused on the terrorist ideology. It is likely that this person spends much of their time with peers, groups, or the organization sharing the ideology, or possibly on terrorist-related websites where they are being radicalized. Counterradicalization would focus on mitigating the effects of radicalization by preventing the individual from engaging in violence, disengaging them from the terrorist group, and helping them reintegrate back into society.

The third approach, antiradicalization, can be targeted toward people in the general public, particularly individuals who may be vulnerable to joining an extremist group, including adolescents, people with mental health problems, and individuals who have experienced family upheaval. These types of counter-terrorist measures can take place in schools or offices or as part of community programs as a way to prevent individuals seeking out meeting their needs from extremist groups. These programs can provide information about the radicalization process, the early signs of radicalization, and detecting at-risk individuals; it also highlights vulnerable populations.

Who Is at Risk of Radicalization?

Many readers might be surprised to learn that violent extremist views can occur among any religious, political, or social views. Contrary to popular belief, no religious, social, or political group is immune to violent extremism. Furthermore, people across varying socioeconomic statuses, levels of education, cultures, and nationalities can be influenced by radical ideology. In fact, it is noted that many individuals within well-known Middle Eastern terrorist groups, such as Al Qaeda and the Islamic State of Iraq and Syria (ISIS), come from middle- to high-income families and possess high levels of education. Often, these individuals have specializations in aeronautical engineering, chemistry, and information technology; skills that are used to meet specific goals of the organization, particularly with planning violent attacks. However, there are certain factors that could lead individuals to become involved with violent extremism and radical ideology.

Typically, individuals who have experienced inequality or discrimination, have been marginalized, or have experienced historical or social injustices are those likely to join groups that promote a radical ideology. This is particularly true when the group ideology involves a fight toward justice for past grievances, or promises a better future for these individuals. Often, individuals who have experienced family upheaval, loneliness, or low self-esteem are among those that recruiters prey on. Terrorist recruiters look for individuals that lack family support, have financial troubles, or are in need of peer relationships, as these individuals are more susceptible to accepting extremist ideology without critically thinking about the damage the ideology could create. People who are vulnerable to joining terrorist organizations often do so to feel a sense of community and belonging, to feel better about themselves, or to gain a sense of purpose and meaning in life, and often believe that their cause will create positive change in the world. Often, recruiters rely on adolescents and young adults who are at risk of isolation, low self-esteem, and low self-worth, and have not fully developed skills to critically challenge these extreme ideologies. Furthermore, if these young people come from dysfunctional families, they run a high risk of being radicalized. Given that many terrorist organizations recruit through the Internet, young people who are isolated and spend long hours online also run the risk of becoming radicalized.

Additionally, people with mental health conditions are also susceptible to joining violent extremist groups. People with autism spectrum disorders, substance use disorders, schizophrenia and other psychotic disorders, and severe mood disorders are those that engage in a lot of black-and-white thinking, may become obsessive with the ideology, and may not have the mental capacity to consider the consequences of the ideology they are following. Furthermore, these ideologies may appeal to people with mental health problems, especially if they feel stigmatized by others and do not have family or friends watching out for their well-being. It has been noted that the "lone-wolf" terrorists tend to have a higher prevalence of mental health conditions than those who have joined a terrorist organization.

Early Signs of Radicalization

As mentioned earlier, no individual becomes indoctrinated into an extremist ideology overnight. The process of radicalization takes place over time, sometimes even over a few years. During that time, the individual will begin to exhibit some emotional, cognitive, and behavioral signs of change. While emotional and cognitive changes may not be easy to detect, they can be detected through the individual's observable behavior. The following can be signs that the suspected individual is in the early to midstages of radicalization:

- Suddenly breaks relationships with family members and other previously important relationships
- Isolates themselves from family and friends, or becomes detached and withdrawn
- Suddenly drops out of school, quits their job, or has conflicts at school or the workplace
- Becomes disrespectful to parents and siblings, or has anger outbursts with family members
- Makes antisocial comments about carrying out violent acts, engages in arguments with other people in defense of their ideology, asks inappropriate questions, or makes inappropriate statements about violence
- Exhibits changes in behavior related to their food, clothing, or finances and may present a decline in appearance
- Has an unhealthy use of the Internet and/or regularly visits websites and social media promoting radical or extremist views
- Increasingly makes statements about the extremist ideology and may refer to apocalyptic theories about the world

If these changes are observed in an individual, family members and friends should intervene. It is important to build a strong support system for this individual and to determine what physical or psychological needs this person has. It is important that violent extremism prevention should be done through education, and that prevention measures should be taken at the family and community level. Prevention programs need to be implemented at schools, workplaces, and community centers, and as part of PSA campaigns.

Approaching Individuals Undergoing Radicalization

Just as there is no one-size-fits-all approach to the deradicalization process, there is no clear solution to approaching an individual who is gradually becoming radicalized by an extremist group or ideology. However, there are certain steps that one can take that can make the individual more likely to critically evaluate the negative impact of the ideology that they have become involved in. If you have notice a family member or friend exhibiting some of the early warning signs, the following steps can be taken:

1. Have a family member or friend (someone the individual trusts or has a close relationship with) take the time to talk to the person about concerns they have about the behavioral changes they have noticed. It is important not to involve every family member or friend known to the person, or stage a large intervention, as doing so could make the person feel defensive. Rather, having one or two trusted people initially intervene could let the person know that others are concerned and care about them, without making them feel cornered. It is also important that the initial discussion is carefully planned with the family member or friend before engaging the person. It could be helpful to review information on the extremist viewpoint in order to understand the misconceptions and myths.

2. When engaging in a discussion, listen closely to the person in a nonjudgmental manner and keep an open mind about their responses. By doing so, you can find out what is really going on with the person and will be able to understand the person's context. Being nonjudgmental can be very difficult, particularly when the person's ideology condones violence toward others. However, doing so is critical in truly understanding the person's new worldview. Below are some ways you can express open-mindedness:

   a. Allow the person to express their argument, rather than interrupting them.

b. When voicing your concern, avoid condemning the person during the discussion (e.g., do not respond with "you can't say that" or "you can't think like that" if a person indicates that people must be persecuted or hurt in the name of their ideology). Doing so will make the person become defensive and feel that they cannot express themselves. (Note: It is important to know that doing so does not condone their statements; it merely lets them know that they are being heard by someone.)

c. Just as many people view themselves as serving a just cause, so do people who are in the process of being radicalized. It is important not to use labels such as "terrorist" or "extremist" when talking to them or to label their group as such.

d. Do not overinterpret controversial statements as necessarily being a sign of violent extremism.

e. Avoid making yourself the individual who is "right" or the authority in the discussion. Instead, by listening to and reflecting those statements made by the individual, you can indicate to the person that you understand what they are trying to express.

f. Ensure that both you and the person involved are given an equal opportunity to express your viewpoint.

g. Ask for a clarification if you do not understand what the person has expressed; doing so lets the person know they are being heard. Some ways of asking for clarification include

    i. Can you explain what … means as I did not understand?
    ii. Give me an example of …
    iii. Can you tell me why you think this is important?
    iv. Where did you learn that from?
    v. What is the difference between … and … ?

3. As previously mentioned, the process of radicalization takes time to completely make an individual actually engage in violence. People who are in the initial stages of radicalization are likely to believe in the ideology, though they may not agree that they should resort to violence. In fact, data suggest that while many individuals may sympathize with terrorist organizations, most of them are not willing to actually engage in violence. When individuals believe in an ideology that proposes violence, while at the same time believing that they should not harm other individuals, they experience a conflict of beliefs, a phenomenon known as "cognitive dissonance." Simply put, cognitive dissonance occurs within an individual when they experience a conflicting set of beliefs causing them to be in an anxious state. In order to reduce the anxiety they experience, members of terrorist groups put recruited individuals through conditions to reduce this dissonance. During early stages of radicalization, family members and friends can counter these effects by engaging in the opposite behaviors.

Condition	Solution
Isolating themselves from others	Providing opposing perspectives from nonorganization members; having them socially engage with others
Holding a good vs. evil worldview	Engaging in discussions to illustrate that many of the world's problems are complex and that many problems do not have a clear answer
Justifying any means to bring about an ideal society	Emphasizing concerns that violence is not the answer to bringing about an ideal society
Believing that terrorists can make a change	Highlighting that terrorists' roles cause harm and violence to others
Experiencing a society that feels unjust	Consider ways in which individuals can fight unjust states and governments without the use of violence

By utilizing some of these solutions, family members and friends can counter the radical ideology the person holds. It is important that when debating these statements or ideas, the person making these statements is not attacked; rather, it is the ideology being critiqued. By demonstrating that you can consider other positions and viewpoints on the issue, the person being recruited can learn that they can do the same. Over time, the person engaging in these discussions is likely to critically think and analyze their beliefs, and in considering other viewpoints, they could change their radical position.

4. Rather than simply engaging the recruited individual in a critical discussion alone, it is important to have them involved in community activities. If their ideology states that a certain group of people (race, orientation, gender, ethnicity, etc.) are to be persecuted, have that individual socialize with a person or people from that diversity group; doing so can help humanize the people within the group and may make the individual realize that their ideology is harmful. If the terrorist organization holds an extreme view within a specific religion, it could be helpful to have the radicalized individual meet with religious experts to engage in a discussion about what their belief system states. Likewise, if the ideology is based on a radical political worldview, it is helpful to have the individual meet with experts (political scientists, professors, etc.) in the field to engage in a discussion about the origin of this viewpoint.

5. Given that individuals who are recruited into terrorist groups are often those experiencing isolation, low self-esteem, and emotional problems, it is

important to address these concerns. By having the individual engage in community activities, they are more likely to feel a sense of belonging and less isolated. It could also be helpful to have the individual meet with a counselor or mental health provider to address any emotional or mental health problems they may be experiencing so that they are able to get their needs met.

Early Prevention at the Workplace

Given that employees spend much of their time at the workplace, it is possible that changes in an employee's behavior can be detected by an employer or other colleagues. An employee may be involved in possible terrorist-related activities if they begin to exhibit some of the early warning signs (mentioned above), or if they start to make concerning statements or act differently than they previously used to. This is not to say that the early warning signs are a definite indication of terrorism; rather, they could be an indication of other life stressors that person may be experiencing. However, involvement in a radicalized group should not be completely ruled out, particularly if the individual begins making concerning statements that resemble extreme political or religious dogma. At this point, the employer may have doubts about this person and may want to pay close attention to that employee.

While it is important for an employer to be attentive to any behavioral changes noted in a suspected employee, the employer needs to know the difference between monitoring and spying on their employees. The distinction between the two can depend on the employee's job description, the type of organization they are working at, and the time and place of monitoring. Typically, an employer can set up video cameras at the workplace, review company e-mail accounts, monitor the employee's workplace computer and Internet activity, and have another employee monitor the suspected employee's behavior at the workplace.

With regard to audio recording, employers can be subject to strict laws, which can vary across different states. More specifically, employers are legally unable to record telephone calls of their employees without the consent of the employee. Furthermore, the employer will need to determine whether the state they are working in is a single-party consent state or a dual-consent state, as the former would require only the employee's consent, whereas the latter would require both parties to consent. It is best recommended that employers state via company policy that all phone calls are recorded, as well as notify all other parties that phone calls will be recorded. Video recordings, on the other hand, have fewer legal restrictions, although the bigger concern is the audio component of the video recording as there may be laws applicable to the audio component of videos. Typically, if the video footage does not contain any audio, employers should have no concerns with legal restrictions.

Privacy infringement is another issue that may arise from video surveillance at the workplace. An employer must be able to discern whether the video surveillance is appropriate and does not overstep their employees' privacy. Typically, video surveillance within the confines of the office would be considered appropriate, whereas tracking the employee outside of office hours would be deemed as spying. It would seem that the legal restrictions regarding surveillance may come down to common sense. However, sometimes the solution to employee surveillance may not always be clear. For example, it would be considered highly inappropriate and an invasion of people's privacy if one was to install cameras in the washroom. However, if a suspected employee is engaging in crimes in the washroom, such as making phone calls to other terrorist group members or Internet surfing terrorist-related information on a pocket device, the lines of privacy may be blurry. While there may not be specific answers to every employee situation, it is best recommended that every employer or organization consider getting legal consultation regarding these issues before engaging in surveillance, as doing so would provide the employer with the best advice within the legal confines of their existing state laws.

Recognizing Suspicious Behavior in Public

Research has not been able to identify terrorist characteristics by which suspicious people can be accurately identified. The best way terrorists can be identified before their attack is by close observation of their behaviors, body language, and physical appearance. This can be done by people working in security, employees of public transportation, and any ordinary citizen who can pay close attention to suspicious-looking people at the workplace, schools, public arenas, important landmarks, or buildings. Typically, if members are working toward attacking a public place, they are likely to examine the area carefully in order to successfully execute the attack. Therefore, some of the behavioral cues to watch out for are

- Making multiple visits to the same location over a period of time
- Making repeated entrances and exits from a building
- Visiting a metro or train station but not actually using it for transportation
- Taking photographs of the location or building
- Drawing diagrams or making notes of the location
- Inquiring about the security systems within the area
- Working in groups
- Avoiding eye contact with others
- Presenting with a weak story if questioned about their presence or immediately running away when confronted
- If working in groups, special attention should be paid to people using mobile phones with one another in the same area

Terrorists who are about to execute their attack in a public place will exhibit signs that they are about to engage in a violent attack.

These include

- Presenting with physical signs of anxiety or nervousness (i.e., trembling, increased sweating, appearing physically ill, avoiding people in uniforms, breathing heavily, nail-biting, pacing, excessive yawning, rubbing their hands, wearing a nervous expression on their face, and repeatedly touching their face)
- Constantly fidgeting, looking for the time on a clock or watch, or scanning the area
- Wearing inappropriate, oversized/loose-fitting clothing, making them look larger in size, e.g., wearing a heavy coat on a warm day
- Appearing in a trance, unresponsive, distant, or inattentive
- Having wires exposed from their clothing or a from a bag they are carrying
- Continually patting themselves (e.g., suicide bombers tend to pat themselves if they are wearing a bomb vest)
- Wearing a disguise (this might not be very noticeable, but close attention could reveal fake facial hair or glasses)
- Maintaining a rigid posture with their arms close to their sides
- Keeping their hands in their pockets
- Keeping their hands cupped (this can indicate them holding a triggering device)
- Holding large and bulky bags closely to themselves
- Maintaining an awkward or ungainly position as if wearing something uncomfortable
- Repeatedly mumbling to themselves when standing outside a building, facility, or crowded location (i.e., repeating a prayer)

It is important to highlight that one or a couple of these indicators do not necessarily suggest that the person will engage in a terrorist attack; the greater the number of indicators, the higher the likelihood that the person being observed is a threat. If the person has presented with sufficient indicators that are deemed suspicious, one of the following measures can be taken: (1) calmly approach them and strike up a casual conversation or (2) report the person to security or public transport personnel or a uniformed officer.

If you decide to approach the person, it is advised to greet the person in a friendly manner and casually inquire if the person needs help. By asking the individual an open-ended question, you are allowing the person to respond with information that requires them to go beyond saying yes or no. Below are some open-ended questions or statements a person could use to start a conversation with the suspect at hand:

- Hello. What's going on?
- What can I help you with today?
- Where are you going today?
- What are you looking for?
- That's a nice coat. Where did you get it? (if the person is wearing a bulky coat)

- That's interesting. What are you working on? (if drawing or taking notes of the location)
- You look ill. How can I help you? (if the person exhibits physical signs of nervousness)
- You look like you could use some help carrying that. (gesture to help with carrying the person's bag)

Typically, any person would respond in a friendly way. However, if the suspected person is a terrorist, the confrontation will lead them to provide evasive answers or even respond aggressively. The person may also present with more nervous behaviors, such as blinking quickly, stammering when responding, avoiding eye contact, responding in a higher vocal pitch, or excessively clearing their throat. If this person continues to appear suspicious, it is best to report them to a law enforcement agency, authority of transportation, or nearby security personnel.

Chapter 11

Track II: Profiling and CounterAction*

Martin Luther King Jr., in his "Loving Your Enemies" speech at the Dexter Baptist Church, November 17, 1957, once said, "Darkness cannot drive out darkness: only light can do that. Hate cannot drive out hate: only love can do that."

Yet other related authors and books may have proclaimed the same or similar philosophical messages: Mahatma Gandhi, the Dalai Lama, Jesus of Nazareth, Margaret Thatcher, Martin Luther, Sai Baba, and scripture from the Holy Torah, the Holy Bible, the Holy Quran, the *Bhagavad Gita*, Buddhism, and Al MuwaHiddoun principles (the foundation of the three Abrahamic faiths taught by Jethro, chief of the Midians, book of Exodus), among many others.

The message of love is not romantic, as some would believe, when drenched in modern-day media, print, and broadcast, which boast wealth at the expense of human decency and dignity. Entertainment seems to gain with sex, profanity, and aggression, leaving the ignorant viewer with a lack of intellectual, emotional, and social wisdom.

The alternative meaning of love in the task is belonging: a sense of connectedness, free from provoking bias, igniting prejudice. Love fosters the basis for trust and respect, allowing for mutual support and leading to friendship, or at least an acquaintance among all people.

---

* Portions of this chapter were previously published in the article "A Dysfunctional Nation and Its People: Becoming Functional," self-published and copyright by Raymond Hamden, and reproduced in various publications.

Could those, the accused and those convicted of terrorism, be victims of educational systems based on bigotry and favoritism? Or could media deliberately send messages of hatred and annihilation to those they believe to be undesirables?

This is not a "Kum ba yah" moment.

What we learned from the majority of the accused was that their family, community, and cultural history was contributory to their current state of psychosocial pursuits. Many were oppressed by society and their governments due to socioeconomic status, race, creed, professional skills, educational level, divorced parents, single parents, and other factors.

A dysfunctional nation and community were noted, with citizens believing that they were treated unfairly and with no equality. These are the people who feared rejection, abandonment, and neglect. Many were treated unethically by authorities, not given equivalent opportunities, and may have been ostracized by peers and others in school or the workplace.

There are four realities that are present in the stressed-out or very injurious nation. People do not know who they are, or they have a false picture as to who they are; they do not sustain their relationships through deep friendship, defenses are used repeatedly, and contentment skills are minimal. Contentment skills are those abilities to sustain long-term relationships, intra- and intercommunity (Knowles & Sabourin, 2008). Failed or dysfunctional states have proliferated across the world, as states suffer from a sovereignty gap that facilitates growth in drug, terrorism, and human trafficking and results in ethnic conflict, genocide, disease, and absolute poverty (Kraeger, 2011). When a nation is in pain and stress, psychological defenses arise. Psychological defenses have two purposes: to give pleasure and to avoid pain.

In political psychology, professionals want to walk through pain so that citizens can discover a true positive identity. Oftentimes, leadership comfort can go deeper than the pain.

The principles of an unhealthy nation are:

> Trust is at a lower level of suspicion.
> Belonging is blind loyalty (Fletcher, 1958).
> Joy is having a life preoccupied with activity.
> Peace is absence of emotion.
> It is your leader's job to make happiness in the in-group.
> It is the other person's fault.
> If they change, we will be happy.
> Don't know what others feel!

In dysfunctional nations, citizens suffer from a lack of empathy, subsequently leading to aggressive behavior (Chaux, Molano, & Podlesky, 2009).

Become emotional or cold and callous! In countries where there are issues pertaining to multiethnic populations, alongside sociological and political problems, especially those of smaller countries, there is a lack of intolerance among the citizens (Andre-Vincent, 1994).

Ignore differences of opinion.
Talk about the person; don't dialogue.
Bring up past failures to help the other person
understand how wrong they are. Confront; don't negotiate!
Use addictions to lessen pain.

These principles are not painted on the walls, but are the implicit assumptions that govern relationships between people of a nation. As these assumptions work themselves out, the relationships become more and more strained. Due to the pain and stress, as often as not, addictive behaviors among citizens arise to kill the pain. The nation cannot endure pain.

Relational Isolation

If friendships developed among the citizens, it was during the years of youth and adulthood. The defense of social isolation did two things: first, it decreased the pain, and second, it gave some pleasure in that they found ways to be preoccupied.

They did not realize the deep loneliness present in this nation. Nor did they recognize the losses of positive worth. They lacked the opportunity to develop contentment skills and discover the pleasures of affection. Nor did they receive the greatest gift of all, a positive picture of themselves and their respective communities, which was supposed to be given by their leadership and government-at-large.

Other defenses are used in the dysfunctional or stressed-out nation. The citizens learn to use evasion and develop a façade. "Practiced amiability" is one way to describe this. On the surface, a friendly smile is present, while underneath there is nonentity. Emotions are not being experienced from years of repression.

Often this is very confusing for a person from a healthy community who engages someone from a stressful community background. Initially, the person with practiced amiability may seem quite charming. After interaction, when the healthy citizen seeks trust and respect, he or she is in for quite a surprise. The closer the attempts, the more anxious the other becomes.

Some will use the self-indulgent activities as a defense for anxiety over intimacy. Anxiety may be due to the lack of contentment skills. The activity gets one out of the perceived vulnerable situations, preoccupation to avoid the issues, and most importantly, an insecure citizen does not have to deal with the challenges of feared relationships. When this phenomenon is unresolved, then eventually there will be separation and misperception of dubious intentions from the other.

Some defenses are social addictions in nature. The in-group concept can be a means to eliminate the pain of cross-community fears. At the same time, these supply a false sense of pleasure. What they really do is deaden the pain of the lack of national protection and give perceived pleasure of security within the smaller community.

When one deals with the issue of in-group psychology, one has to go beyond the surface problem. The real issue is the pain and anxiety of a nation's insecurity. Often pain is deeply present because of the person's family and community background. Therefore, the government and leadership that can reduce the fears can sometimes also ease the need for small-community security.

Researchers have found that some people are social addiction resistant. As they researched the citizens, they found a common factor. Many of them came from content nations, and they had deep sense of feeling worthwhile. They had a positive identity.

The persons who succumbed to social-addictive systems were different. Often they came from stressful communities and nations. Lacking a positive identity or any identity at all, their resistance was low. The observers of troubled citizens and their leaders said that inevitably the people of troubled areas seldom seemed to smile, and they carried a mental scorecard to keep track of their citizen's failures. They were always critical of their citizens.

Unfortunately, even religion can be used as a defense (Kay et al., 2010; Pargament & Park, 1995). On the one hand, it provides a means of getting out of the community and preoccupying oneself. On the other hand, religious experiences can be used to induce pleasure in order to escape pain. Religion, however, was not meant to be used in this fashion.

A person's identity is negatively affected. It can be affected in one of two ways. The first way is that the person will not have a clear or positive picture of who he or she is within the nation. In a chaotic nation, neither accurate nor appreciative insights are shared. That being the case, the individual at the very best will not have a clear sense of citizenship. At worst, he or she will have a deeply negative instinctive view of who he or she is.

People of a dysfunctional government suffer the
fear of rejection, abandonment, and neglect.

Profiling Strategies

The psychological profiling of a terrorist is "primarily concerned with the recognition and identification of patterns and habits of behavior in an individual offender and between offenders committing similar crimes" (Swart, 2016). Furthermore, it is an "educated attempt to provide investigative agencies with specific information about the type of individual who committed a certain crime" (Gerberth, 1981). A profiler provides counter-terrorism agencies with a psychological evaluation of a terrorist's observable behavior at the crime scene that could "provide valuable clues to their personal lives and characteristics (e.g. background and childhood, marital and relationship status, age, gender, race, physical appearance and build, temperament, intelligence, organization, social skills, psychopathology, fantasies, fears and avoidance situations, sexual preferences, criminal history, religious beliefs, and employment)" (Swart, 2016). These are essential information in establishing an attempt to direct an investigation. "Through behavior based profiling and analyzing a collection of items collected from a suspect, psychological profiling may able to offer an interrogator with an appropriate plan for interviewing strategies and gives suggestions about items the offenders may possess" (Sahito, Zahman, & Slany, 2013).

Profiling in the criminal environment is used to identify a suspect involved in the most serious criminal investigations, such as serial cases of murder, multiple murders, or sexual assault. It has also been used in cases of stalking, extortion, kidnapping, product tampering, arson, bombing, espionage, and terrorism (Swart, 2016). However, profiling terrorists is different than profiling criminals. As Wilkins and Brown (2009) described, terrorists are indeed "uncommon" criminals as they are masters of evasion and disguise and take their religion, nationality, and politics very seriously. Citing Wilkins and Brown (2009), Sahito et al. (2013) state that "terrorists profiling attached such proclivities as revenge, religious and social suppression, submission to conventionalism, the displacement of anger onto others, internal guilt, aspirations of toughness, bravado and authoritarian and attracted in the promise of virgins in the hereafter." Sometimes, terrorists represent a perplexing mix of ethnic, economic, and social backgrounds and are likely to be travelers or immigrants (Wilkins & Brown, 2009).

A criminal behavior is unique and unusual and has a psychological driver that suits criminal profiling methods (Swart, 2016). The more sequential the indicators are, the more likely they are "precursor events" that fit a past pattern of known psychological traits that make a recognizable attack vector, which is a warning (Cynthia, 2004). Some criminologists associate this pattern with the term *modus operandi*. According to Swart (2016), "modus operandi—or MO—literally translates to 'method of operation' in Latin. In the context of a criminal investigation, the term describes an offender's habits and methods of committing a criminal act, preventing its detection, and/or facilitating escape." Per Cynthia (2004) as cited by Sahito et al., an "interrogator can analyze the terrorist's habits by comparing the current and previous terrorist acts and much like what used to be called indications and warnings during scanning process that can predict future possible attacks as well as probable sites of terrorist attacks" (Sahito, Zaman, & Slany, 2013). Thus, through the analysis of collected data and pieces held by suspected terrorists, it is anticipated that terrorist profiling in an investigation may be a solution to seize terrorists prior their act of terror. The proactive intelligence-gathering approach of psychological profiling of terrorists directs law enforcement and counter-terrorism agencies to discern mysterious and volatile perpetrators.

Profiling Targets

Prior to interrogation, it is imperative to understand that each terrorist is different with unique personality characteristics or psychopathology. For one type of terrorist, one approach may be operational, but it is a stern mistake to presume that all terrorists will respond to the identical interviewing strategy (Borum, 2004). The logic that drives terrorist profiling efforts is that terrorists can be identified in comparison to a societal population through the observation of noticeable, indicating traits and behavioral patterns. The three most well-known approaches to terrorist detection utilize racial-physical, psychopathological, and socioeconomic attributes as profiling parameters (Rae, 2012).

> Such as to divide terrorist profiling in different categories to steer clear of oversimplified thinking about individual terrorist or groups as either-or a psychological phenomenon or a political phenomenon in the creation of interrogation protocols. These categories are (a) Individual profiling, (b) Group profiling and (c) Organization profiling & (d) Racial, gender and age profiling. (Sahito, Zaman, & Slany, 2013)

Individual Profiling

Through the analysis of the personal history of terrorists, a terrorist personality is anticipated to be discovered that would indicate the individual's willingness to "commit espionage or sabotage, try to overthrow the government, commit terrorist acts, or otherwise engage in acts that would endanger national security" (Siggins, 2002). In addition, there are several factors that may indicate behavioral patterns leading to creating a possible terrorist profile, some of which are socioeconomic and psychopathological (Rae, 2012).

Socioeconomic Profiling

"This strand of terrorist profiling relies on the premise that terrorist proclivity can be ascertained through information on an individual's social status, education, livelihood and marital status, amongst other factors" (Rae, 2012).

Denoeux and Carter (2009) elaborated various socioeconomic background of a terrorist.

> Certainly, the cadres of violent extremist movements—and, specifically, the architects of the most spectacular and deadliest terrorist attacks—have come from fairly privileged backgrounds. Though there are a few partial exceptions to this pattern (e.g., the IRA, ETA, and neo-Nazi groups in the United States), terrorism (especially at the level

of leaders and key activists) traditionally has been an overwhelmingly middle class, and, in several cases (e.g., West Germany and Italy during the 1970s), even an upper-middle class endeavor. By the same token, terrorists traditionally have been highly educated individuals—though variations do exist based on the overall ideological orientation of the groups involved (i.e., with the exception of violent Jewish extremists in Israel, far- left terrorists have tended to be better educated than their counterparts on the extreme right).

These instances depict the fluctuating demographic dimensions that may change with time and place. This illustrates that terrorism, "in part at least, is concomitant to the political environment, and, therefore, it is expectable that as social and economic circumstances evolve, so does the composition of the terrorist demographic. It can be concluded that a successful attempt to profile the terrorist must recognize that its assessment is both ephemeral and context-specific" (Rae, 2012).

Pathological and Psychological Profiling

This approach believes in a fundamental relation between psychopathological behavior and terroristic inclination. "The presence of certain exhibited personality traits or traumatic life experiences is believed to be suggestive of a propensity towards terrorism" (Rae, 2012). A number of psychologists have associated violent behavioral patterns with the presence of mental trauma, sexual deprivation, and/or an oppressive formative atmosphere in the perpetrator's past (Alex, 2005; James, 2008; Reid & McEllistrem, 1998). Sahito et al. note that it is "challenging for law enforcement agencies to develop useful psychological profiles" (Saihto, Zaman, & Slany, 2013), especially for detained terrorist who have not been interviewed or who have not been identified. Below the various classifications and personality categories are detailed.

1. Narcissistic personality
   Citing Borum (2004), Sahito et al. affirm that "interrogators can extract information from these personalities by treating the person with a certain degree of respect and deference that can appeal to his self-inflated egotism. Interrogators should ask them a number of questions during scanning and act impressed by letting them know they are the 'big fish' agencies have been after" (Sahito, 2013).
2. Paranoid personality
   Investigators should piece together some coherent threads of evidence by spinning a theory of the case in yes or no questions during scanning that can later be independently corroborated (Turvey, 2011). This mitigates the distrust that can seep into interviews or interrogations due to the fact that these personalities are inherently distrusting and suspicious.

3. Antisocial personality

These individuals are power seekers and thus are often able to rise in the ranks of groups. They often serve as the "muscle" of the organization and can be assassins or soldiers. They are often impulsive and exploitative and have little loyalty. As such, investigators can exploit this self-serving nature. Deals can be cut with these individuals in exchange for intelligence; however, care must be taken as they can seek to manipulate interrogators and offer up false or misleading information. As such, information obtained should be carefully validated (Sahito, 2013; Turvey, 2011).

4. Borderline personality

These suspects have changeable allegiances, and while they can often work their way up into high-ranking roles, they can also be utilized to turn over intimate details, if they can be convinced that their help will "right the wrong" that's happened to them. A note of caution is that the individual can likewise, and with equal vehemence, turn on the authorities if they feel slighted, rejected, or otherwise misused (Sahito, 2013; Turvey, 2011).

5. Avoidant personality

Interrogators can earn their support and can get information in proportion to the amount of security provided to the suspect. Interrogators should employ a simple and non confrontational style of questions in scanning and should focus on specific questions that allow the suspect to answer yes or no in a piecemeal fashion (Wilkins & Brown, 2009).

6. Histrionic personality

Criminals and extremist groups often enlist these individuals as media representatives or "front men" due to their inherent need for attention. Smart investigation methods can induce the histrionic suspect to barter valuable intelligence for the promise of a positive spotlight. The information obtained with an investigatory asset should be independently corroborated due to suspect's tendency for self-aggrandizement and embellishment (Gerberth, 1981; Turvey, 2011).

7. Schizoid personalities

Schizoid suspects often respond best, and reveal information, in response to simple and precise questions during interrogation. They often exhibit more eccentric, bizarre, or detached behavior in addition to delusional thinking. As such, while they can reveal useful information and intelligence, their delusional perspectives can at times limit and mitigate its usefulness (Turvey, 2011; Sahito, 2013).

Group Profiling

Methods used to determine profiles of individuals oftentimes can similarly be applied to better understand various groups. And as Sahito et al. state, "It is also important to consider the social influence and motivational basis involved in recruitment of new members to terrorist organization and their indoctrination into terrorist ideology" (Sahito, Zaman, & Slany, 2013).

> The fact that it is not possible to generalize about the profile of popu-
> lations susceptible to violent extremism across countries, regions, and
> time periods does not mean that one cannot detect such a profile for a
> particular country, location, or movement at a given historical juncture.
> Of course, all the relevant caveats apply, including:
>
> ■ One should not assume that a clear-cut profile will necessarily
>   emerge from the evidence (indeed, in many cases, that will not
>   be the case).
> ■ In countries where extremist groups are not particularly active or
>   are just emerging, there will be too few extremists to make profil-
>   ing a meaningful exercise. It is critical that the analyst not gen-
>   eralize from too small a sample of terrorists or violent incidents.
> ■ Profiles can change quickly.
> ■ The background of members of a given movement in a particular
>   country or region may be very different from the background of
>   militants in that same movement in other locations.
>
> Still, early on in the analysis of a particular country, the analyst
> should seek to determine whether one or several subsets of the overall
> population appear to be particularly susceptible to involvement in
> violent extremist activities. That this may be the case should not be
> assumed, but it should not be ruled out either. Given that resources for
> assessment, design, and programming are limited, it is useful, when
> appropriate, to target the communities, institutions, and settings that
> appear to be producing a disproportionate percentage (relative to the
> overall population) of violent extremists. One way to pinpoint the
> at-risk population is to gain a broad sense of extremist groups oper-
> ating in the country, examine the profiles of those who have been
> recruited or who appear to support violent extremists, and deter-
> mine whether there are commonalities among them. (Denoeux &
> Carter, 2009)

Organization Profiling

"It is important to consider that profiling of all these organizations is mutually rein-
forcing and interdependent. The organization depends on group-level processes of
socialization and indoctrination, which in turn operate on individual psychologies

that contribute their motivation to the advancement of terrorist causes and for group survival. These three different profiles operate in concert to further boost the culture of terrorism" (see also Sahito, Zaman, & Slany, 2013; Stephen, 2002).

Denoeux and Carter (2009) stated that "violent extremist (VE) organizations may be better understood by seeking to place them along three different, but related, continua."

1. The first continuum would help focus on the extent to which these organizations (and the individuals within them) are driven by specific grievances and negotiable goals, as opposed to very broad ideological (especially religious) appeals and nonnegotiable demands. The more a given organization appears to be motivated by fairly narrow grievances, and the more it is pursuing objectives that at least are clearly defined and theoretically attainable, the closer it is to one end of that continuum. By contrast, if it is fueled primarily by ideological fervor and absolutist goals that are all encompassing and nebulous (and subject to frequent changes), and/or if these goals do not lend themselves to negotiations and compromise, the closer it is to the other end of that same continuum.

2. The second continuum would examine VE organizations from the perspective of the theater(s) in which they believe their struggle is being waged, and within which they operate. Near one end of the continuum, one would find "territorialized" organizations that tend to articulate "local" or "nationalist" demands, and/or seek to achieve control over a particular territory (which they may claim as their own and view as being occupied). Close to the other end of the continuum, one would find "de-territorialized" VE organizations that see themselves as being engaged in a global, worldwide struggle that knows no frontiers.

3. The third continuum would distinguish among VE organizations according to the extent to which they are embedded in the communities they claim to represent. Whether such organizations actively seek, and do enjoy, broad-based support from the local population is important for both analytical and counter-terrorism purposes.

Violent extremist organizations that are driven by broad ideological appeals and/or religious fervor are rarely attached to a particular territory, and they tend to view their struggle as a global one. They display a greater propensity to be "transnational" in nature, and they often aim to bring violence to an ever-expanding number of theaters of operation. Meanwhile, organizations that are embedded in the community often are territorialized ones as well (by definition, since they seek and receive the support of a given local community), while organizations driven by global agendas are often superimposed on, and alien to, the communities within which they operate. (Denoeux & Carter, 2009)

Racial, Gender, and Age Profiling

Jonathan Rae most succinctly characterizes racial profiling:

> The crudest and most egregious method of profiling terrorists is to identify potential malfeasors based on racial characteristics. Implicit in racial profiling is the logic that individuals of a certain race are, as a general rule, more likely to commit acts of terrorism. In this thinking, ethnicity and alienage are viewed as adequate demographic divisions to be proper subjects of scrutiny. (Rae, 2012)

Ellman (2003) states that "[profiling] on the basis of race and comparable factors, is both discriminatory and foolish. Arabs and Muslims—to name the two most obvious targets for such reactions today—are part of the American mainstream. Many are citizens. The vast majority … are altogether innocent of any connection with terrorism. Meanwhile, some people who are not Arabs … have apparently joined our enemies in Al Qaeda."

Another absolute element to profile terrorists is biological gender. The dominance of male terrorists should not be overstated, despite having numerical superiority show that the 9/11 attack and most terrorist attacks in Pakistan were and are done by male terrorists (Rae, 2012). Moreover, Hudson (1999) writes that "women have played prominent roles in numerous urban terrorist operations in Latin America, and that the female terrorists during the siege of the Palace of Justice were among the fiercest fighters." As with ethnicity, the use of gender as a main factor in terrorist profiling is undermined by the influence of exceptions against the generalization. An efficient terrorist profile must be developed using meters that are more clearly analytical of terrorist behavior and lessen the malfeasor population to a probable size for secondary screening (Rae, 2012, 66).

> The issue of age discrimination in terrorist profiling is also an example of the failure to limit the filtering of a large population into a manageable group. There is no definitive age group that terrorists fall into. Although the majority of terrorists are in their early twenties, the average age of several terrorist groups is considerably lower (Benmelech & Berrebi, 2007). Hudson (1999) writes that the LTTE had 'many members in the 16 to 17 year-old age level and even members who were preteens'. At the other extreme, the leadership hierarchies of terrorist organizations tend to be markedly older than the mean age. Both Osama bin Laden and Carlos Marighella were in their late 50's when they were killed. The new head of Al Qaeda, Ayman al-Zawahiri, turned sixty last year. When the FBI's Most Wanted Terrorists list was published in 2001, the average age of the 22 individuals listed was 37 years old. In light of this variety, it is clear that age is a problematic

measure of profiling potential terrorists. It is of interest to note at this point that while race, age and gender profiling in the criminal context—such as the routine searching of young black males by police patrols—is condemned as prejudiced, unconstitutional or institutionally racist, the equivalent usage in the terrorism context is largely overlooked by the general public.

Profiling is not a perfect profession as yet.
With experience to develop evidence-based measures,
we may find strategies that will objectively guide us to
effectively communicate, understand without prejudice,
and address the terrorists and acts of terrorism
for correction as well as prevention ...

Bibliography

AFP. (2010, April 19). Donkey bomb kills three children in Afghanistan. *Herald Sun.* Retrieved from http://www.heraldsun.com.au/archive/news/donkey-bomb-kills-three-children-in-afghanistan/news-story/b970bf1e81fe160f84c8c32cef77eec3.

Alex, S. (2005). Links between terrorism and drug trafficking: A case of narcoterrorism? *International Summit on Democracy, Terrorism and Security, and Political Violence, 10*(2), 53–85.

Ali, A. (1997). *The Meaning of Holy Quoran.* Beltsville, MD: Amana Publications.

Alison, L. J., Alison, E., Noone, G., Elntib, S., & Christiansen, P. (2013). Why tough tactics fail and rapport gets results: Observing Rapport-Based Interpersonal Techniques (ORBIT) to generate useful information from terrorists. *Psychology, Public Policy, and Law, 19*(4), 411.

Alison, L., & Alison, E. (2017). Revenge versus rapport: Interrogation, terrorism, and torture. *American Psychologist, 72*(3), 266.

Allen, R. E. (1986). *The Oxford Spelling Dictionary.* Oxford: Clarendon Press.

Al-Qaisi, M. (2011, February 14). Iraq accuses al-Qaida of using mentally ill man to kill 33 civilians in Samarra. *Al Shofra.* Retrieved from http://al-shorfa.com/cocoon/meii/xhtml/en_GB/features/meii/features/main/2011/02/14/feature-02.

Amabile, T., Ross, L., & Steinmetz, J. (1977). Social roles, social control, and biases. *Social-Perception Processes, 35*(7), 485–494.

American Psychiatric Association. (2013). *Diagnostic and Statistical Manual of Mental Disorders (DSM-5).* Washington, DC: American Psychiatric Publishing.

Anderson, C. A., & Bushman, B. J. (2002). Human aggression. *Annual Review of Psychology, 53*, 27–51.

Ansari, H. (1984). The Islamic militants in Egyptian politics. *International Journal of Middle East Studies, 16*(1), 123–144.

Apple, R. W., Jr. (1985). Thatcher urges the press to help 'starve' terrorists. *New York Times.* Retrieved from https://www.nytimes.com/1985/07/16/world/thatcher-urges-the-press-to-help-starve-terrorists.html.

Avolos, H. (2005). *Fighting Words: The Origins of Religious Violence.* New York: Prometheus.

Azar, E. E., Jureidini, P., & McLaurin, R. (1978). Protracted social conflict; theory and practice in the Middle East. *Journal of Palestine Studies, 8*(1), 41–60.

Balthazard, P. A., Cooke, R. A., & Potter, R. E. (2006). Dysfunctional culture, dysfunctional organization. *Journal of Managerial Psychology, 21*(8), 709–732

Bandura, A. (1977). *Social Learning Theory.* Englewood Cliffs, NJ: Prentice Hall.

Bandura, A. (1986). *Social Foundations of Thought and Action: A Social Cognitive Theory.* Upper Saddle River, NJ: Prentice Hall.

Banse, R., Koppehele-Gossel, J., Kistemaker, L. M., Werner, V. A., & Schmidt, A. F. (2013). Pro-criminal attitudes, intervention, and recidivism. *Aggression and Violent Behavior, 18*(6), 673–685.

Benmelech, E., & Berrebi, C. (2007). Human capital and the productivity of suicide bombers. *Journal of Economic Perspectives, 21*(3), 223–238.

Berkowitz, L. (1969). The frustration-aggression hypothesis revisited. In L. Berkowitz (Ed.), *Roots of Aggression: A Re-Examination of the Frustration-Aggression Hypothesis* (pp. 1–28). New York: Atherton Press.

Blackwood, L., Hopkins, N., & Reicher, S. (2013). I know who I am, but who do they think I am? Muslim perspectives on encounters with airport authorities. *Ethnic and Racial Studies, 36*(6), 1090–1108.

Blair & Rita Justice. (1990, April). *The Abusing Family*. Oklahoma City: Insight Books.

Bond, M. (1992). An empirical study of defensive styles: The Defense Style Questionnaire. In G. E. Vaillant (Ed.), *Ego Mechanisms of Defense* (pp. 127–158). Washington, DC: American Psychiatric Press.

Borum, R. (2003). Understanding the terrorist mindset. *FBI Law Enforcement Bulletin, 72*(7), 7–10.

Borum, R. (2004). *Psychology of Terrorism*. Tampa, FL: University of South Florida.

Borum, R. (2015). Assessing risk for terrorism involvement. *Journal of Threat Assessment and Management, 2*(2), 63–87.

Bouchek, C. (2008). Saudi Arabia's "soft" counterterrorism strategy: Prevention, rehabilitation and aftercare. Washington, DC: Carnegie Endowment for International Peace.

Bowen, W. R. (2003). *Japan's Dysfunctional Democracy: The Liberal Democratic Party and Structural Corruption*. New York: M. E. Sharpe

Bradshaw, J. (1986). Bradshaw *On: The Family: A New Way of Creating Self-Esteem*. Houston: John Bradshaw.

Brannan, D. W., Esler, P. F., & Anders Strindberg, N. T. (2001). Talking to "terrorists": Towards an independent analytical framework for the study of violent substate activism. *Studies in Conflict and Terrorism, 24*(1), 3–24.

Brown, T., & Murphy, M. (2011). Self-respect, self-confidence and self-esteem: Psychoanalytic and philosophical implications for higher education. *Cliopsy, 6*, 43–51.

Bushman, B. J., & Anderson, C. A. (2002). Violent video games and hostile expectations: A test of the general aggression model. *Personality and Social Psychology Bulletin, 28*(12), 1679–1686.

Chaux, E., Molano, A., & Podlesky, P. (2009). Socio-economic, socio-political and socio-emotional variables explaining school bullying: A country-wide multilevel analysis. *Aggressive Behavior, 35*(6), 520–529.

Chiaramonte, P. (2014). ISIS seizes uranium from lab: Experts downplay 'dirty bomb' threat. Fox News. Retrieved from http://www.foxnews.com/world/2014/07/10/isis-seize d-uranium-compounds-from-lab-experts-downplay-threat.html.

Chipkin, I. (2003). 'Functional' and 'dysfunctional' communities: The making of national citizens. *Journal of Southern African Studies, 29*(1), 63–82.

Choudhury, T., & Fenwick, H. (2011). The impact of counter-terrorism measures on Muslim communities. *International Review of Law, Computers & Technology, 25*(3), 151–181.

Clarke, C., & Milne, R. (2012). National evaluation of the PEACE investigative interviewing course. Police research award scheme. Retrieved December 30, 2017, from https:// so-fi.org/wp-content/uploads/peaceinterviewcourse.pdf.

Clark, S. (2014, December 11). Ex-CIA director Petraeus says he opposed detainee torture. *Wall Street Journal*. Retrieved from http://www.wsj.com/articles/ex-cia-director-petraeus-says-he-opposed-torture-1418314146.

Clutterbuck, L. (2015). Deradicalization programs and counterterrorism: A perspective on the challenges and benefits. Understanding Deradicalization: Pathways to Enhance Transatlantic Common Perceptions and Practices, Middle East Institute.

Committee of Ministers of the Council of Europe. (2000). *Role of Early Psychosocial Intervention in the Prevention of Criminality*. Strasbourg, France: Council of Europe Publishing.

Connor, W. (1978). A nation is a nation is a state, is an ethnic group is a …. *Ethnic and Racial Studies*, *1*(4), 377–400.

Corrado, R. R. (1981). A critique of the mental disorder perspective of political terrorism. *International Journal of Law and Psychiatry*, *4*(3–4), 293–309.

Corte, L. D. L., & Giménez-Salinas, A. (2009). Suicide terrorism as a tool of insurgency campaigns: Functions, risk factors, and countermeasures. *Perspectives on Terrorism*, *3*. Retrieved from http://www.terrorismanalysts.com/pt/index.php/pot/article/view/62/html.

Cramer, P. (2015). Defense mechanisms: 40 years of empirical research. *Journal of Personality Assessment*, *97*(2), 114–122.

Craparo, G., Schimmenti, A., & Caretti, V. (2013). Traumatic experiences in childhood and psychopathy: A study on a sample of violent offenders from Italy. *European Journal of Psychotraumatology*, *4*, 21471.

Crenshaw, M. (1986). The psychology of political terrorism. In M. G. Hermann (Ed.), *Political Psychology: Contemporary Problems and Issues* (pp. 379–413). London: Jossey-Bass.

Crenshaw, M. (2000). The psychology of terrorism: An agenda for the 21st century. *Political Psychology*, *21*(2), 405–420.

Cynthia, G. (2004). *Anticipating Surprise: Analysis for Strategic Warning*. Lanham, MD: University Press of America.

Davis, L. E., LaTourrette, T., Mosher, D. E., Davis, L. M., & Howell, D. R. (2003). Individual preparedness and response to chemical, radiological, nuclear, and biological terrorist attacks. RAND Corporation. Retrieved from https://www.rand.org/pubs/monograph_reports/MR1731.html.

De Castella, K., & McGarty, C. (2011). Two leaders, two wars: A psychological analysis of fear and anger content in political rhetoric about terrorism. *Analyses of Social Issues and Public Policy*, *11*(1), 180–200.

De Quervain, D. J., Fischbacher, U., Treyer, V., Schellhammer, M., Schnyder, U., Buck, A., & Fehr, E. (2004). The neural basis of altruistic punishment. *Science*, *305*(5688), 1254–1258.

Deloughery, K. (2013). Simultaneous attacks by terrorist organisations. *Perspectives on Terrorism*, *7*. Retrieved from http://www.terrorismanalysts.com/pt/index.php/pot/article/view/312/html.

DeMause, L. (2002). The childhood origins of terrorism. *Journal of Psychohistory*, *29*, 340–348.

Denoeux, G., & Carter, L. (2009, February). U.S. AID guide to the drivers of violent extremism. Retrieved from https://pdf.usaid.gov/pdf_docs/Pnadt978.pdf.

Department of Defense. (2010). Department of Defense Dictionary of Military and Associated Terms.

Department of Homeland Security. (n.d.). Chemical attack warfare agents, industrial chemicals, and toxins. *News and Terrorism: Communicating in a Crisis.* Retrieved from https://www.dhs.gov/xlibrary/assets/prep_chemical_fact_sheet.pdf.

Departments of the Army and the Air Force. (1990). Military operations in low intensity conflict. Retrieved from www.bits.de/NRANEU/others/amd-us-archive/FM100-20%2890%29.pdf.

Desai, R. (2013). Terrorism. Retrieved from http://drrajivdesaimd.com/2013/06/01/terrorism/.

Drake, C. J. M. (1998). The role of ideology in terrorists' target selection. *Terrorism and Political Violence, 10*, 53–85.

D'Souza, D. (2009, November 16). On religion and terrorism. *The News*, 1–5.

Dulles, A. (2002). Christ among religions. *American Magazine, 186*(3), 1–9.

Ellie, B., & Nur, L. (2015). A new approach? Deradicalization programs and counterterrorism. New York: International Peace Institute.

Elliot, H., & Sapsted, D. (1988). Muammar Gaddafi ordered Lockerbie bombing, says Libyan minister. NewsCore Online& Bomb Fear in UK's Worst Air Disaster. *The Times (London).* Retrieved April 12, 2011, from http://www.news.com.au/breaking-news/muammar-gaddafi-ordered-lockerbie-bombing-says-libyan-minister/story-e6frfku0-1226011070628&; http://www.timesonline.co.uk/tol/archive/tol_archive/article6794731.ece

Ellman, S. J. (2003). Racial profiling and terrorism. *New York Law School Law Review, 46*, 688.

Evans, J. R., Meissner, C. A., Ross, A. B., Houston, K. A., Russano, M. B., & Horgan, A. J. (2013). Obtaining guilty knowledge in human intelligence interrogations: Comparing accusatorial and information-gathering approaches with a novel experimental paradigm. *Journal of Applied Research in Memory & Cognition, 2*, 83–88.

Everly, G. S. J. (2003). Psychological counterterrorism. *International Journal of Emergency Mental Health, 5*(2), 57–59.

Faure, G., & Zartmann, W. (2009). Negotiating with terrorists: A mediator's guide. IIASA Policy Brief 6.Laxenburg, Austria: International Institute for Applied Systems Analysis, AUT.

Faure, G., & Zartman, W. (2011). *Negotiating with Terrorists: Strategy, Tactics and Politics.* London: Routledge.

Fenoglio, J. (2016). Résister à la stratégie de la haine. *Le Monde.* Retrieved from http://www.lemonde.fr/idees/article/2016/07/27/resister-a-la-strategie-de-la-haine_4975150_3232.html.

Finn, J. L., & Jacobson, M. (2008). Social justice. In T. Mizrahi & L. E. Davis (Eds.), *The Encyclopedia of Social Work.* Washington, DC: NASW and Oxford University Press. Retrieved from http://www.oxfordreference.com/view/10.1093/acref/9780195306613.001.0001/acref-9780195306613-e-364.

Fischer, P., Kastenmüller, A., & Greitemeyer, T. (2010). Media violence and the self: The impact of personalized gaming characters in aggressive video games on aggressive behavior. *Journal of Experimental Social Psychology, 46*, 192–195.

Fischer, P., Postmes, T., Koeppl, J., Conway, L., & Fredriksson, T. (2011). The meaning of collective terrorist threat: Understanding the subjective causes of terrorism reduces its negative psychological impact. *Journal of Interpersonal Violence, 26*(7), 1432–1445.

Fiske, S. T., & Taylor, S. E. (1991). *Social Cognition* (2nd ed.). New York: McGraw-Hill.

Fletcher, T. W. (1958). The nature of administrative loyalty. *Public Administration Review, 18*(1), 37–42. Retrieved from http://www.jstor.org/stable/973733.

Gadarian, S. K. (2010). The politics of threat: How terrorism news shapes foreign policy attitudes. *Journal of Politics, 72*(2), 469–483.

Gallimore, T. (2004). Unresolved trauma: Fuel for the cycle of violence and terrorism. In C.Stout (Ed.), *Psychology of Terrorism: Coping with the Continuing Threat, Condensed Edition*(pp. 67–93). New York: Praeger.

Gbaffou, B. C. (2008). Democratic system? Lessons from practices of local democracy in Johannesburg. *Critical Dialogue—Public Participation in Review* Local councillors: Scapegoats for a dysfunctional participatory, 26–33.

Gerberth, V. (1981). Psychological profiling. *Law and Order 29*, 46–49.

Gigerenzer, G. (2006). Out of the frying pan into the fire: Behavioral reactions to terrorist attacks. *Risk Analysis: An Official Publication of the Society for Risk Analysis, 26*(2), 347–351.

Gilligan, J. (2003). Shame, guilt and violence. *Social Research, 70,* 1149–1180.

Goldman, A., & Blinder, A. (2017, January 16). F.B.I. arrests wife of killer in Orlando mass shooting. *New York Times*. Retrieved from https://www.nytimes.com/2017/01/16/us/politics/noor-salman-arrested-orlando-shooting-omar-mateen.html.

Goodman-Delahunty, J., Martschuk, N., & Dhami, M. K. (2014). Inter- viewing high value detainees: Securing cooperation and disclosures. *Applied Cognitive Psychology, 28,* 883–897.

Grohol, J. M. (2016, May 17). 15 common defense mechanisms. *Journal of Medicine*, Retrieved June 19, 2018, from https://psychcentral.com/lib/15-common-defense-mechanisms/.

Gudjonsson, G. H. (2011). False confessions and correcting injustices. *New England Law Review, 46,* 689.

Hamden, R. H. (2002). The retributional terrorist—Type 4. In C. E. Stout (Ed.), *The Psychology of Terrorism: Clinical Aspects and Responses* (pp. 165–193). Westport, CT: Greenwood Publishing Group.

Hamersma, R. (2005, Oct 22). Dysfunctional nation. *National Post*. Retrieved from http://ezproxy.aus.edu/login?url=http://search.proquest.com/docview/330417418?accountid=16946

Hartwig, M., Granhag, P. A., Strömwall, L. A., & Vrij, A. (2005). Detecting deception via strategic disclosure of evidence. *Law and Human Behavior, 29,* 469–484.

Heskin, K. (1980). *Northern Ireland: A Psychological Analysis.*Dublin: Gill and Macmillan.

Heskin, K. (1985). Political violence in Northern Ireland. *Journal of Psychology, 119*(5), 481–494.

Hoffman, B. (2006). *Inside Terrorism*. New York: Columbia University Press.

Holmes, R. M., & DeBurger, J. (1988). *Serial Murder: Studies in Crime, Law and Justice* (Vol. 2). Newbury Park, CA: Sage.

Horgan, J. (2014). *The Psychology of Terrorism*. New York: Routledge.

Hudson, R. A. (1999). *The Sociology and Psychology of Terrorism: Who Becomes a Terrorist and Why?* (p. 53). Washington, DC: Library of Congress.

Hudson, R. A. (2018). *Who Becomes a Terrorist and Why? The Psychology and Sociology of Terrorism*. New York: Skyhorse Publishing.

Hudson, R. A. (1999). The sociology and psychology of terrorism: Who become a terrorist and why? Retrieved from https://www.loc.gov/rr/frd/pdf-files/Soc_Psych_of_Terrorism.pdf.

Human Rights Watch (2003). The legal prohibition against torture. Retrieved December 30, 2017, from https://www.hrw.org/news/2003/03/11/legal-prohibition-against-torture.

Iyer, A., Webster, J., Hornsey, M. J., & Vanman, E. J. (2014). Understanding the power of the picture: The effect of image content on emotional and political responses to terrorism. *Journal of Applied Social Psychology, 44*(7), 511–521.

James, J. (2008). *Blood that Cries Out from the Earth: The Psychology of Religious Terrorism.* Oxford: Oxford University Press.

Jetter, M. (2014). Terrorism and the media. IZA Discussion Paper No. 8497. Retrieved from http://ftp.iza.org/dp8497.pdf.

Jetter, M. (2017). The effect of media attention on terrorism. *Journal of Public Economics, 153*, 32–48.

Jones, A. M., & Brimbal, L. (2017). Lay perceptions of interrogation techniques: Identifying the role of Belief in a Just World and Right Wing Authoritarianism. *Journal of Investigative Psychology and Offender Profiling, 14*(3), 260–280.

John E. Reid & Associates, Inc. (n.d.). Retrieved December 28, 2017, from http://www.reid.com/educational_info/critictechnique.html.

Justice, B., & Justice, R. (1990). *The Abusing Family.* New York: Insight Books.

Kagan, R., & Schlosberg, S. (1989). *Families in Perpetual Crisis.* New York: W. W. Norton & Company.

Kaplan, E. (2006). Q&A: Terrorists and the Internet. *New York Times.* Retrieved from https://archive.nytimes.com/www.nytimes.com/cfr/international/slot2_030606.html?_r=1&oref=slogin.

Kaslow, F. W. (1996). *Handbook of Relational Diagnosis and Dysfunctional Family Patterns.* Hoboken, NJ: Wiley-Interscience.

Kay, A. C., Shepherd, S., Blatz, C. W., Chua, S. N., & Galinsky, A. D. (2010). For God (or) country: The hydraulic relation between government instability and belief in religious sources of control. *Journal of Personality and Social Psychology, 99*(5), 725–739. doi:10.1037/a0021140.

Khelghat-Doost, H. (2017). Women of the Caliphate: The mechanism for women's incorporation into the Islamic State (IS). *Perspectives on Terrorism, 11*, 17–25.

Kerr, M. E., & Bowen, M. (1988). *Family Evaluation.* New York: W. W. Norton & Company.

Kfir, N. (2002). Understanding suicidal terror through humanistic and existential psychology. *Psychology of Terrorism, 1*, 143–157.

Kingsley, O. (2010). Religion and terrorism: A socio-historical reconsideration. *Journal of Alternative Perspectives in the Social Sciences, 2*(2), 550–576.

Knoll, J. L. (2010). The "pseudocommando" mass murderer: Part I, the psychology of revenge and obliteration. *Journal of the American Academy of Psychiatry and the Law, 38*, 87–94.

Knowles, M., & Sabourin, M. (2008). Psychology and modern life challenges: The 2nd Middle East and North Africa Regional Conference of Psychology, Amman, Jordan, 2007. *International Journal of Psychology, 43*(2), 130–139. doi:10.1080/00207590801983967.

Kobrin, N. H. (2016). Nobody born a terrorist, but early childhood matters: Explaining the jihadi's lack of empathy. *Perspectives on Terrorism, 10*. Retrieved from http://www.terrorismanalysts.com/pt/index.php/pot/article/view/546/html.

Kraeger, P. (2011). Nation building: How dysfunctional nations can achieve legitimacy and prosperity in the twenty-first century, *71*(2), 313–316. Retrieved from http://onlinelibrary.wiley.com/doi/10.1111/j.1540-6210.2011.02347.x/full.

Kraeger, P. (2011). Nation building: How dysfunctional nations can achieve legitimacy and prosperity in the twenty-first century. *Public Administration Review, 71*(2), 313–316.

Kruglanski, A. W., Crenshaw, M., Post, J. M., & Victoroff, J. (2007). What should this fight be called? Metaphors of counterterrorism and their implications. *Psychological Science in the Public Interest: A Journal of the American Psychological Society, 8*(3), 97–133.

Kydd, A. H., & Walter, B. F. (2006). The strategies of terrorism. *International Security, 31*(1), 49–80.

Lankford, A. (2011). Requirements and facilitators for suicide terrorism: An explanatory framework for prediction and prevention. *Perspectives on Terrorism, 5.* Retrieved from http://www.terrorismanalysts.com/pt/index.php/pot/article/view/requirements-and-facilitators/html.

Larsen, S. (2007). *The Fundamentalist Mind: How Polarized Thinking Imperils Us All.* Wheaton, IL: Quest Books.

Lassiter, G., & Pinegar, S. (2013). Interrogation. *Criminology.* doi:10.1093/OBO/9780195396607-0180.

Leo, R. A. (2013). Why interrogation contamination occurs. *Ohio State Journal of Criminal Law, 11*, 193.

Leo, R. A., & Drizin, S. A. (2010). The three errors: Pathways to false confession and wrongful conviction. In G. D. Lassiter & C. A. Meissner (Eds.), *Police Interrogations and False Confessions: Current Research, Practice, and Policy Recommendations* (pp. 9–30). Washington, DC: American Psychological Association.

Logothetis, N. K., Pauls, J., Auguth, M., Trinath, T., & Oeltermann, A. (2001, July). A neurophysiological investigation of the basis of the BOLD signal in fMRI. *Nature, 412*(6843), 150–157.

López-Rousseau, A. (2005). Avoiding the death risk of avoiding a dread risk: The aftermath of March 11 in Spain. *Psychological Science, 16*(6), 426–428.

Lowe, D., Turk, A., & Das, D. (2013). *Examining Political Violence: Studies of Terrorism, Counterterrorism* (pp. 84–85). Boca Raton, FL: CRC Press.

MacDonald, S., Keeping, Z., Snook, B., & Luther, K. (2017). Do not lie to me, or else: The effect of a turncoat warning and rapport building on perceptions of police interviewers. *Journal of Police and Criminal Psychology, 32*(3), 263–277.

Madigan, M. L. (2017). *Handbook of Emergency Management Concepts: A Step-by-Step Approach.* Boca Raton, FL: CRC Press.

Mallot, R. W. (1988). Rule governed behavior and behavioral anthropology. *Behavior Analyst, 11*(2), 181–203.

Marcus, G. E. (2002). *The Sentimental Citizen: Emotion in Democratic Politics.* PA: Pennsylvania State University Press.

Martin, G. (2009). *Understanding Terrorism: Challenges, Perspectives and Issues.* Thousand Oaks, CA: SAGE Publications Ltd.

Maxey, L. (2018). Terrorists stalk dark web for deadlier weaponry. *Cipher Brief.* Retrieved from https://www.thecipherbrief.com/terrorists-stalk-dark-web-deadlier-weaponry.

McLemore, C. W., & Brokaw, D. W. (1987). Personality disorders as dysfunctional interpersonal behaviour. *Journal of Personality Disorders, 1*(3), 270–285

Meissner, C., Redlich, A., Bhatt, S., & Brandon, S. (2012). Interview and interrogation methods and their effects on investigative outcomes. *Campbell Systematic Reviews, 8*(13), 1–49.

Meloy, J. R. (2004). Indirect personality assessment of the violent true believer. *Journal of Personality Assessment, 82*, 138–146.

Meloy, J. R., & McEllistrem, J. E. (1998). Bombing and psychopathy: An integrative review. *Journal of Forensic Sciences, 43*(3), 556–562.

Meloy, J. R., Mohandie, K., Hempel, A., & Shiva, A. (2001). The violent true believer. *Journal of Threat Assessment, 1*(4), 1–15.

Moore, T. E., & Fitzsimmons, C. L. (2011). Justice imperiled: False confessions and the Reid technique. *Criminal Law Quarterly, 57*, 509.

Morgan, C. A., Wang, S., Mason, J., Southwick, S. M., Fox, P., Hazlett, G., ... Greenfield, G. (2013). Hormone profiles in humans experiencing military survival training. In S. E. Hyman (Ed.), *The Science of Mental Health: Stress and the Brain* (Vol. 9, pp. 25–35). New York, NY: Routledge.

Morrison, A. (1997). *Shame: The Underside of Narcissism.* Piscataway, NJ: Routledge.

Moston, S., & Engelberg, T. (2011). The effects of evidence on the outcome of interviews with criminal suspects. *Police Practice and Research, 12,* 518 –526.

Mowatt-Larssen, R. (2010, January 25). Al Qaeda's pursuit of weapons of mass destruction. *Foreign Policy.* Retrieved from http://foreignpolicy.com/2010/01/25/al-qaedas-pursuit-of-weapons-of-mass-destruction/.

Mueller, G. O. W. (1961). The law relating to police interrogation privileges and limitations. *Journal of Criminal Law, Criminology, and Police Science,* 2–15.

Mueller, J. (2005). Six rather unusual propositions about terrorism. *Terrorism and Political Violence, 17*(4), 487–505.

Multi-National Corps. (2007, April 6). Suicide vehicle detonates outside police checkpoint. *Wayback Machine.* Retrieved from https://web.archive.org/web/20090912161746/http://www.mnf-iraq.com/index.php?option=com_content&task=view&id=11185&Itemid=128.

Murgia, M. (2017). Twitter says almost 300,000 terrorist accounts taken down in first half of 2017. *Financial Times.*Retrieved from https://www.ft.com/content/035a2e13-622f-346f-bad4-c8e7be7ace09.

Myers, D. G. (2000). The funds, friends, and faith of happy people. *American Psychologist, 55*(1), 56–67

Napier, N. J. (1990). *Recreating Your Self: Help for Adult Children of Dysfunctional Families.* New York: W. W. Norton & Co.

Nesser, P., & Stenersen, A. (2014). The modus operandi of jihadi terrorists in Europe. *Perspectives on Terrorism, 8.* Retrieved from http://www.terrorismanalysts.com/pt/index.php/pot/article/view/388.

Neuharth, D. (1999). *If You Had Controlling Parents: How to Make Peace with Your Past and Take Your Place in the World.* Collingdale, PA: DIANE Publishing Company.

Ohmae, K. (1993). The rise of region state. *Foreign Affairs, 72*(2).

Okoro, K. (2017). Islamic jurisprudence and unity of Nigeria: A socio-historical reconsideration. *Open Journal of Philosophy,7*(4), 467–483. doi:10.4236/ojpp.2017.74025.

O'Mara, S. (2015). *Why Torture Doesn't Work: The Neuroscience of Interrogation.* Cambridge, MA: Harvard University Press.

Orlando, J. (2014). Interrogation techniques. Office of Legislative Research. Retrieved December 28, 2017, from https://www.cga.ct.gov/2014/rpt/2014-R-0071.htm.

Pargament, K. I., & Park, C. L. (1995). Merely a defense? The variety of religious means and ends. *Journal of Social Issues, 51*(2), 13–32. doi:10.1111/j.1540-4560.1995.tb01321.x.

Rae, J. (2012). Will it ever be possible to profile the terrorist? *Journal of Terrorism Research, 3.*

Ramsdell, L. (2004). *The Ties That Bind: Questioning Family Dynamics and Family Discourse in Hispanic Literature.* Lanham, MD: University Press of America.

Rapoport, David C. (1984) "Fear and Trembling: Terrorism in Three Religious Traditions" *American Political Science Review, 78*(3), 655–677.

Rapoport, D. C. (1984). Fear and trembling: Terrorism in three religious traditions. *American Political Science Review, 78,* 658–677.

Reid, E., Qin, J., Chung, W., Xu, J., Zhou, Y., Schumaker, R., Sageman, M., & Chen, H. (2004). Terrorism knowledge discovery project: A knowledge discovery approach to addressing the threats of terrorism. In *International Conference on Intelligence and Security Informatics* (pp. 125–145). Berlin: Springer.

Renken, B., Egeland, B., Marvinney, D., Mangelsdorf, S., & Sroufe, L. A. (1989). Early childhood antecedents of aggression and passive-withdrawal in early elementary school. *Journal of Personality*, *57*(2), 257–281.

Ripley, A. (2002). The case of the dirty bomber. *Time*. Retrieved from http://content.time.com/time/nation/article/0,8599,262917,00.html.

Russano, M., Narchet, F., Kleinman, S., & Meissner, C. (2014). Structured interviews of experienced HUMINT interrogators. *Applied Cognitive Psychology*, *28*, 847–859.

Ruggiero, T. E. (2007). Televisa's Brozo: The jester as subversive humorist. *Journal of Latino-Latin American Studies*, *2*(3), 1–15.

Rummel, R. J. (1994). Power, genocide, & mass murder. *Journal of Peace Research*, *31*, 1–10.

Rummel, R. J. (1995). Democracy, power, genocide, & mass murder. *Journal of Conflict Resolution*, *39*.

Rummel, R. (1997). *Death by Government*. Piscataway, NJ: Transaction Publishers.

Sahito, F., Zaman, S., & Slany, W. (2013). Terrorist profiling as a counterinsurgency strategy: Applying the concept to law enforcement. *International Journal of Innovation and Applied Studies*, *4*(2), 274–285.

Salib, E. (2003). Suicide terrorism: A case of folie à plusieurs? *British Journal of Psychiatry*, *182*(6), 475–476.

Saylor.org. (n.d.). The fundamental attribution error. Retrieved from https://www.saylor.org/site/wp-content/uploads/2010/12/The-Fundamental-Attribution-Error.pdf.

Schbley, A. (2003). Defining religious terrorism: A causal and anthological profile. *Studies in Conflict & Terrorism*, *26*(2), 105–134. Retrieved from http://dx.doi.org/10.1080/10576100390145198.

Schifrin, N. (2009, November 25). Mumbai terror attacks: 7 Pakistanis charged. ABC News. Retrieved from http://abcnews.go.com/International/mumbai-terror-attacks-pakistanis-charged/story?id=9176592.

Schmid, A., & Jongman, A. (2005). *Political Terrorism*. Piscataway, NJ: Transaction Publishers.

Stoop, D., & Masteller, J. (1997). *Forgiving Our Parents, Forgiving Ourselves: Healing Adult Children of Dysfunctional Families*. Raleigh, NC: Regal.

Shaw, E. D. (1986). Political terrorists: Dangers of diagnosis and an alternative to the psychopathology model. *International Journal of Law and Psychiatry*, *8*(3), 359–368.

Siggins, P. (2002). Racial profiling in an age of terrorism. Retrieved from http://www.scu.edu/ethics/publications/ethicalperspectives/profiling.html.

Silke, A. (1998). Cheshire-cat logic: The recurring theme of terrorist abnormality in psychological research. *Psychology, Crime and Law*, *4*(1), 51–69.

Silke, A. (2001). The devil you know: Continuing problems with research on terrorism. *Terrorism and Political Violence*, *13*(4), 1–14.

SIU School of Medicine. (n.d.). Overview of potential agents of biological agents. SIU School of Medicine: Internal Medicine. Retrieved from https://www.siumed.edu/im/overview-potential-agents-biological-terrorism.html.

Skitka, L. J., & Mullen, E. (2002). The dark side of moral conviction. *Analyses of Social Issues and Public Policy*, 35–41.

Speckhard, A., & Yayla, A. S. (2015). Eyewitness accounts from recent defectors from Islamic State: Why they joined, what they saw, why they quit. *Perspectives on Terrorism, 9*. Retrieved from http://www.terrorismanalysts.com/pt/index.php/pot/article/view/475.

Stanton, N. (2009). *Mastering Communication* (5th ed.). Basingstoke: Palgrave Macmillan.

Stein, A. (2006). *Prologue to Violence: Child Abuse, Dissociation and Crime.* Mahwah, NJ: Analytic Press.

Stephen, E. (2002). Racial profiling and terrorism. *New York Law School Law Review, 46*, 675.

Stohl, M. (1984). The superpowers and international terror. Paper presented at the Annual Meeting of the International Studies Association, Atlanta, March 27–April 1.

Strategic Foresight Group (2007). *An Inclusive World.* Mumbai, India: Sundeep Waslekar.

Swart, J. (2016). *Criminal Profiling:Revealing the Science of Behavior.* Detroit: Lilit Publishing.

Tanay, E. (1987). Pseudo-political terrorism. *Journal of Forensic Sciences, 32*(1), 192–200.

Taylor, M. (1991). *The Fanatics: A Behavioral Approach to Political Violence.* London: Brasseys.

Terrorism. (n.d.). In Princeton Word Net Search. Retrieved fromhttps://www.wordnetweb.princeton.edu/perl/webwn.

The Gottman ratio: Discipline vs. praise at the wayback machine (archived July 2011).

The Psychology of the terrorist. (n.d.). Retrieved from http://www.neuromaster.com/LOCsocpsyterrorism/spt_06.htm

Thórisdóttir, H., & Jost, J. T. (2011). Motivated closed-mindedness mediates the effect of threat on political conservatism. *Political Psychology, 32*(5), 785–811.

Townsend, E. (2007). Suicide terrorist: Are they suicidal? *Suicide and Life-Threatening Behavior, 37*, 35–49.

Trevithick, P. (2011). Understanding defenses and defensiveness in social work. *Journal of Social Work Practice, 25*, 389–412.

Turvey, B. (2011). *Criminal Profiling: An Introduction to Behavioral Evidence Analysis.* Amsterdam: Elsevier.

Tyler, T. R., Schulhofer, S., & Huq, A. Z. (2010). Legitimacy and deterrence effects in counterterrorism policing: A study of Muslim Americans. *Law & Society Review, 44*(2), 365–402.

United Nations (2004). Report of the Security Council. Retrieved from https://digitallibrary.un.org/record/532566/files/A_59_2EN-.pdf.

United we stand. (1942, July). House Furnishing Review. Retrieved from http://amhistory.si.edu/1942/campaign/campaign24.html.

United States Army. (2006). *Field manual 2.22.-3, Human Intelligence Collector Operations.* Washington, DC: Headquarters, U.S. Army. Retrieved from http://fas.org/irp/doddir/army/fm2-22-3.pdf.

U.S. Commission on National Security in the 21st Century (1999, September 15). New world coming: American security in the 21st century: Supporting research and analysis. Retrieved from http://govinfo.library.unt.edu/nssg/NWR_A.pdf.

Vaillant, G. (1993). *The Wisdom of the Ego.* Cambridge, MA: Harvard University Press.

Vallano, J. P., Evans, J. R., Schrieber Compo, N., & Kieckhaefer, J. M. (2015). Rapport-building during witness and suspect interviews: A survey of law enforcement. *Applied Cognitive Psychology, 29*, 369–380.

Vaillant, G. E. (1992). *Ego Mechanisms of Defense: A Guide for Clinicians and Researchers.* Washington, DC: American Psychiatric Press.

Valencia, M. J., Khatib, H., & Kim, M. S. (2011, February 25). Religion and terrorism: A socio-historical reconsideration. *Eurasia Review News & Analysis*. Retrieved from https://www.eurasiareview.com/25022011-religion-and-terrorism-a-socio-historical-reconsideration/.

Varvin, S., & Volkan, V. D. (2003). *Violence or Dialogue? Psychoanalytic Insights on Terror and Terrorism*. London: International Psychoanalytical Association.

Victoroff, J. (2005). The mind of the terrorist. *Journal of Conflict Resolution*, *49*(1), 3–42.

Vinod, S. (2003). *Dealing with Global Terrorism: The Way Forward*. New Delhi: Sterling Publishers.

Ward, V. (2015). New Oxford University vice-chancellor says U.S. 'over-reacted' to 9/11. *The Telegraph*. Retrieved from https://www.telegraph.co.uk/education/educationnews/11645939/New-Oxford-University-vice-chancellor-says-U.S.-over-reacted-to-911.html.

Weimann, G. (2016). Going dark: Terrorism on the dark web. *Studies in Conflict & Terrorism*, *39*(3), 195–206.

Whitfield, C. (1995). *Memory and Abuse: Remembering and Healing the Effects of Trauma*. Deerfield Beach, FL: Health Communication Inc.

Whitfield, L. C. (1991). *Co-Dependence Healing the Human Condition: The New Paradigm for Helping Professionals and People in Recovery*. Atlanta: Health Communications.

Wilkins Newman, D., & Brown, N. D. (2009). Historical overview and perceptions of racial and terrorist profiling in an era of homeland security. *Criminal Justice Policy Review*, *20*(3), 359–374.

Xing, L., & Jize, Q. (2006). Effective communication key to mutual understanding. *China Daily* (North American ed.), 3.

Additional References

Bandura, A. (2006). Training in terrorism through selective moral disengagement. In J. J. F. Forest (Ed.), *The Making of a Terrorist: Recruitment, Training and Root Causes* (Vol. 2, pp. 34–50). Westport, CT: Praeger.

Hancerli, S., & Durna, T. (2007). Successful police negotiation strategies in terrorism motivated hostage situations. *Understanding & Responding to the Terrorism Phenomenon*, *21*(1), 195–209.

Kruglanski, A. W., Gelfand, M., & Gunaratna, R. (2010). Detainee deradicalization: A challenge for psychological science. *APS Observer*, *23*(1).

Lowther, A., & Lindsay, B. (2009). *Terrorism's Unanswered Questions*. Westport, CT: Praeger.

Luckabaugh, R., Fuqua, H. E., Cangemi, J. P., & Kowalski, C. J. (1997). Terrorist behavior and United States foreign policy: Who is the enemy? Some psychological and political perspectives. *Psychology*, *34*(2), 1–15.

Maikovich, A. K. (2005). A new understanding of terrorism using cognitive dissonance principles. *Journal for the Theory of Social Behaviour*, *35*(4), 373–397.

Monahan, J. (2012). The individual risk assessment of terrorism. *Psychology, Public Policy, and Law*, *18*(2), 167.

Morris, M., Eberhard, F., Rivera, J., & Watsula, M. (2010). Deradicalization: A review of the literature with comparison to findings in the literatures on deganging and deprogramming. Durham, NC: Institute for Homeland Security Solutions.

Okoro, K. (2008). Religion and global conflict: A re-examinations' flash. *A Journal of Philosophy and Religion*, *2*(1), 105–115.

Okoro, K. (2010). Religion and terrorism: A socio-historical reconsideration. *Journal of Alternative Perspectives in the Social Sciences*, *2*(2), 550–576.

Pettigrew, Thomas F. (1979). The ultimate attribution error: Extending Allport's Cognitive analysis of prejudice. *Personality and Social Psychology Bulletin*, *5*, 461–476

Rausch, C. C. (2015). Fundamentalism and terrorism. *Journal of Terrorism Research*, *6*(2), 28. doi:10.15664/jtr.1153.

Senghal, V. (2003). *Dealing with Global Terrorism the Way Forward*. New Delhi: Sterling Publishers.

Stern, J. (2010). Mind over martyr: How to deradicalize Islamist extremists. *Foreign Affairs*, 95–108.

Stout, C. E. (2002). *ThePsychology of Terrorism: A Public Understanding (Psychological Dimensions to War and Peace)*. Westport, CT: Greenwood Publishing Group.

Stout, C. E. (2002). *The Psychology of Terrorism: Clinical Aspects and Responses* (Vol. 2) Westport, CT: Greenwood Publishing Group.

Stout, C. E. (2002). *ThePsychology of Terrorism: Theoretical Understandings and Perspectives* (Vol. 3). Westport, CT: Praeger/Greenwood.

Sukabdi, Z. A. (2015). Terrorism in Indonesia: A review on rehabilitation and deradicalization. *Journal of Terrorism Research*, *6*(2), 36–56.

UNESCO. (2016). A teacher's guide on the prevention of violent extremism. Retrieved from unesdoc.unesco.org/images/0024/002446/244676e.pdf.

Weimann, G. (2016). Terrorist migration to the dark web. *Perspectives on Terrorism*, *10*, 40–44.

Wilkinson, P. (1997). The media and terrorism: A reassessment. *Terrorism and Political Violence*, *9*, 51–64.

Index